D0363749

FAMOUS FIGHTER ACES

FAMOUS FIGHTER ACES

BRYAN PHILPOTT

Patrick Stephens Limited

First published in 1989

British Library Cataloguing in Publication Data

Philpott, Bryan, *1936-*
Famous fighter aces.
1. World War 1. Air operations by fighter
aeroplanes. Pilots
2. World War 2. Air
operations by fighter aeroplanes. Pilots
I. Title
940.4'41

ISBN 1-85260-025-X

Patrick Stephens Limited is part of the Thorsons Publishing Group,
Wellingborough, Northamptonshire NN8 2RQ, England.

Printed in Great Britain by Mackays of Chatham, Kent

1 3 5 7 9 10 8 6 4 2

CONTENTS

ACKNOWLEDGEMENTS

I should like to record my sincere thanks to the following who have unselfishly helped by making their own researches available, loaning material, offering advice, proof reading, translating, and typing letters: Chaz Bowyer, Norman Franks, Chris Shores, Jerry Scutts, Simon Parry, John Foreman, Debbie George, Wendy Sacs of Bison Books Ltd, Rita Ward, Oddy Rada-Ludlow, and Heather Cook. The final selection of aces was my own, and any errors are also mine.

Other sources include the IWM, MoD(Air) AHB, RAF Museum, PRO Kew, Bundesarchiv Koblenz and Freiburg, Deutsche Dienstelle, the library of the Royal Aeronautical Society, *Air Pictorial, Aviation News, Aeroplane Monthly, Aircraft Illustrated Extra, Flypast,* USAF, USMC, USN.

This book is dedicated to Suzy, who was an 'ace' in a different sense of the word, and whose short life was full of happiness and brought joy to many.

WHAT IS AN ACE?

ACE : *n*. the 'one' at dice, cards, dominoes; single point; (sl) very successful fighting airman; person expert at anything.

*T*he simplified dictionary definition quoted sums up the general interpretation of a word that has slipped into everyday everyday use and is much favoured by headline copywriters to emphasize the prowess of a person who has shown a flair for practically any competitive—and sometimes not so competitive—achievement. However, 'What is an ace?' is like the unanswerable question 'How long is a piece of string?', for in many ways the answer depends on the yardstick being used. In the context we are dealing with, it is perhaps therefore advisable to define the parameters that are usually accepted as being those applicable to a very successful fighting airman, although in so doing it would be dangerous to assume that reaching 'ace' status automatically qualifies the recipient to meet the last part of the quoted definition!

Since man first competed against man, the champion or hero accolade has been a vital ingredient of the so-called competitive spirit. In Roman times, the most successful gladiators attracted the largest following, and when the sword gave way to the jousting lists, knights vied with each other to win the fair damsel or even perhaps large slices of the estates of the vanquished knight. Archers travelled for miles to pit their skills against each other at country fairs, and as time moved on this competitive spirit became an essential ingredient of every pastime. It was a natural progression, therefore, that during the Great War, when aerial fighting became part and parcel of modern warfare, people would look to this new dimension to provide them with their champions, who indeed in the early days were often referred to as Knights of the Air. Propagandists were not slow to see the value of creating champions to parade before the civilian population, and although in most cases the military frowned on the practice of idolizing individuals, the die was already cast.

The French and Germans quickly saw the advantages to morale of the 'fighter ace' label, whilst the British were very reluctant to enter into such idolization, much preferring to extol the virtues of teamwork that had been their hallmark since 'the playing fields of Eton' concept had been established. In some cases, as we shall see, they were perfectly correct, and teamwork *was* the key to many an ace reaching the pinnacle of achievement. The French chose five confirmed aerial victories as their criterion, and this has now become accepted as the necessary figure to be classified as an ace. The Germans, however, required ten before they were prepared to bestow the title '*experte*' on their flyers.

It is also necessary at this stage to outline briefly other factors that must be taken into account when considering 'ace' status, although in a work of this size it is not possible to go into every facet in detail.

The broad parameters of the 'ace' system were established during the First World War, and laid the foundations from which the concept grew. Both the French and Germans were particularly fastidious in verifying claims, with independent witnesses and positive identification of wreckage being vital factors. With front lines being fairly static, and combats not taking place at very high altitudes, these criteria were not too difficult to meet. Moreover, the Germans allowed no shared victories, whereas the Allies credited such claims to the unit as well as to each individual pilot involved. It is easy to see, therefore, that individual tallies, at least during the early days of aerial combat, should be eyed with a certain amount of suspicion, especially as aircraft destroyed on the ground were also included. As mentioned earlier, the British did not publicly subscribe to the recognition of individual scores, but citations for awards mentioned aerial victories, so it is not too hard to build up an overall picture. As far as the British were concerned, the terms 'destroyed' and 'out of control' were adopted, both counting as victories, whereas the French, for example, would take the latter as a 'probable' and *not* include it in the score, and the Germans would not even consider it.

In the First World War, the combat area was reasonably static, the aircraft of the combatants were more or less equal in performance and the skills of pilots were in the widest possible sense of a similar standard. It is not too surprising, therefore, that those pilots generally considered to be the leading aces of the German, French and British air services achieved comparable scores, these being as follows:

GERMAN		FRENCH		BRITISH EMPIRE	
von Richthofen	80	Fonck	75	Bishop	72
Udet	62	Guynemer	54	Mannock	68
Lowenhardt	53	Nungesser	45	Collishaw	62

American volunteer airmen had their scores assessed in accordance with the standards adopted by the air force with which they flew, but when America officially entered the war, the French system was used apart from the two squadrons operating under British jurisdiction, so once again generalization can be seen to be dangerous.

Aerial fighting in the First World War was in its infancy, but by the time the Second World War started much had been learned both in practice, in various minor conflicts, and in theory. Much of the latter, compiled from lessons gleaned from the experiences of combatants in the various theatres, very quickly had to be modified when it came to reality.

Aircraft had advanced beyond all recognition from the mounts of the first aces; they were faster, more heavily armed, flew higher and were in general harder to use as effective weapons by average squadron pilots. Once again using the broadest possible brush to paint the canvas, let us consider some of the issues that must be taken into account when it comes to looking at Second World War aces.

Materially there was little change in the scoring methods adopted; the Germans still tended to be extremely fastidious, while the British still refused to adopt any 'official' recognition of the ace system but changed their 'out of control' category to 'probably destroyed', but did not include it in scores. The French, however, made a complete turn-round and counted 'probables' as victories.

In the early days of the war, it seems very likely that the Allies did on some occasions include shared successes as whole numbers, but towards the middle of the conflict a fraction or decimal system was adopted. It is clear, therefore, that in some cases two, three or four pilots might be credited with individual victories thus giving a false picture of their overall scores, whereas later such claims would result as ½, ⅓ or ¼. This should not be considered as an attempt to belittle any ace, because equally there were many occasions when for a variety of reasons claims were not made, or an experienced pilot, flying with a newcomer to his unit, would give the embryo pilot full credit for a victory in which he may well have played an important part. The Americans also counted aircraft destroyed on the ground as part of a pilot's overall total, although during 1944 they leaned strongly towards treating these as separate achievements, and it is not unusual to see the term 'strafing ace' used in some accounts.

The biggest controversy, however, comes within the area of total claims credited to individual pilots, with many of the high-scoring Luftwaffe pilots now being looked at with suspicion. This is a pity, because there can be very little doubt that the totals claimed are authentic and result from unique situations in which Luftwaffe pilots found themselves.

To put this into perspective, it is necessary first to look at the major criteria that affected all pilots at one time or another, before making a close examination of the factors which have pointed the finger of suspicion towards the Luftwaffe.

There are three distinct areas of fighter operations:

DEFENSIVE Where the pilot is fighting over territory that is friendly towards him and is trying to prevent the enemy reaching his objective. If he is shot down unharmed he will not be lost to the defending force and hopefully will soon be back in action.

OFFENSIVE Usually the opposite of the above, involving pilots who are operating over enemy territory or controlled areas trying to achieve air superiority by negating the opposing air force. If shot down they are lost to the enemy.

Examples of the first might be the Battle of Britain and the Battle of Malta, in which the British had the advantage of defending over friendly territory, while the second is exemplified by the daylight defence of the Reich, in which of course the tables were turned. The third area is:

INTRUDER OR NIGHT-FIGHTER FIGHTING In the above-mentioned areas, it was customary for fighter aircraft to operate as composite units ranging from pairs to fours or to squadrons. In this third category they would be more likely to operate as singletons using the cover of darkness, patience and stealth, aided by electronic equipment such as airborne radar, to seek their quarries.

Night fighters introduced an element in the scoring procedures that had not been a major factor in the First World War, and that was the two-man crew. The two-seater scouts of the earlier conflict rarely had any weapons operated by the pilot, so the gunner was the man credited with victories. A Second War legacy of those days was the Boulton Paul Defiant, a descendent of the earlier philosophy of a two-man crew. This turret fighter with four Browning .303 machine-guns had a short and inglorious period as a day fighter in the Second World War before being confined to night fighting, and then only as a stop-gap until specialist aircraft such as the Beaufighter and Mosquito came into service. The policy of giving 'ace' status to gunners was thus short-lived, and it became common practice to award the accolade to the two-man crew or, in the case of the Luftwaffe, sometimes three-man crew, with the emphasis usually on the pilot.

In recent conflicts the wheel has turned again, with the modern fighter's radar operator or weapons systems officer, or to give him the more usual colloquial title 'the guy in the back seat' (GIB), often receiving recognition in his own right.

Whilst on the subject of night fighters, it is worthwhile taking a moment to look at the development of those used in the Second World War. At the start of hostilities, little thought had been given to interception during the hours of darkness. As it became increasingly obvious that daylight bombing was fraught with danger for the bomber crews with all the odds stacked against them, a switch to night bombing became inevitable.

On the British side, early attempts were made to use Spitfires and Hurricanes in the night fighter role, but apart from a few isolated successes the skill required to operate this type of aircraft in darkness was beyond that of the average squadron pilot. The Defiant and Mk 1 Blenheim, equipped with rudimentary airborne interception radar, bridged the gap until the Beaufighter entered service and was later supplemented by the remarkable Mosquito.

The Luftwaffe followed a similar pattern by adapting the Bf 110 two-seater day fighter into a very successful radar-equipped night fighter, which was also supported by a plane which, like the Mosquito, started life as a bomber but by the end of the war had become a jack-of-all-trades, and master of most of them, the Ju 88. Late in the war, the superlative Heinkel He 219 was introduced into squadron service by the Luftwaffe, and this could well have been the ultimate Second World War night fighter, and was certainly the first equipped with ejection seats. In the night fighting role, the Germans also used a two-seater radar-equipped version of the Me 262 jet fighter, but lack of accurate records has so far prevented any true assessment of this aircraft's success in this capacity. It is worth noting, however, that its performance and armament were better than that of the Gloster Meteor NF 11, the first jet-powered night fighter to equip post-war RAF fighter squadrons in 1951, and ironically enough replacing the Mosquito.

The Luftwaffe also made use of single-seater Bf 109s and FW 190s to penetrate bomber streams on clear nights, or when the aircraft were over highly illuminated target areas. Some of these were radar equipped and achieved far greater success than their opposite RAF types used in the same roles earlier in the war, but the reasons for this are not within the scope of this particular narrative. Most night fighters were much more heavily armed than their day fighter brothers, and on many occasions it has been suggested that, certainly as far as the RAF's Bomber Command aircraft such as the Wellington, Stirling, Halifax and Lancaster were concerned, there was virtually no contest. The British 'heavies' had rifle calibre .303 Browning machine-guns in power-operated turrets, the German night fighters had batteries of 20 mm and 30 mm cannon in their noses or gun pods, and the lethal vertical firing Schräge Musik arrangement. These weapons outranged those of the British, and certainly had more devastating fire-power. Once vectored on to a bomber, German fighter pilots could sit well outside the range of its defensive armament and, when satisfied that the crew were not perhaps as vigilant as they might be, swoop in for the kill. On the other hand, if they allowed themselves to be fooled by the bomber and get too close, a burst of .303 ammunition could be just as fatal to them. Many Luftwaffe night fighter veterans are on record as saying that if the bomber crew were alert and started weaving or twisting as soon as they detected the enemy fighter, they would break off the engagement and look for easier prey.

One other interesting factor is that, with radar and heavier armament, the modified Bf 110s and Ju 88s had a very narrow speed differential over the RAF's 'heavies', so if the two or three power turrets fitted to the bombers, the ammunition and men required to operate them had been deleted, the aircraft's overall performance would have been increased to a point where interception purely in a tail chase situation would have been impossible. But that's another story.

Turning back to the question of differences in claims between Allied and Luftwaffe crews, one of the reasons is to be found in the way each air force regarded its operational aircrew. The Allies tended to use their pilots, radar operators and gunners on what has become known as an 'Operational Tour'; this was thirty sorties on bombers as far as the RAF was concerned, and 25 in the USAAC. On fighter squadrons, pilots usually flew a number of operational hours before being 'rested'; this could mean that during their time with a squadron they could well be in the thick of the fighting for fairly extended periods, but on the other hand if they were in a theatre that turned quiet, patrol could follow patrol with very little happening. At the end of the period, unless the pilot was able to extend his tour by fair means or subterfuge, he would be sent as an instructor to a flying school, an Operational Training Unit or an Operational Conversion Unit, or perhaps even into an administrative position where he would 'fly a desk' until returning later to operations. After the problematic days of 1940 when pilots had been in very short supply, such changes became easy to administer, and the flow of new pilots from the schools often limited the total time a man spent in actual operational flying.

In the Luftwaffe it was very different. Once posted to a unit, the crew stayed with it, the only breaks being for standard periods of leave, or recovery from injury. True, some crews had to be removed from the front line to carry out other tasks including instruction, but overall it is true to say that most pilots spent far longer on operations than their opposite numbers. There are of course many other factors. Success on the Russian Front, for example, has often been dismissed since it was considered to have been against much inferior opposition, but this is a gross distortion. Many of the Russian aircraft were handled by extremely competent pilots and would have been more than a handful for any ace, whatever his nationality. Obviously some aircraft were inferior, but the reason for high scores is a combination of many other factors, not least being the close proximity of the opposing front lines, which gave not only a longer period in a potential combat area, but also a shorter transit time to such areas and a shorter time on the ground being refuelled and rearmed. An individual pilot could fly many more sorties on the Russian Front than he would, for example, have been able to in the Battle of Britain. These operational conditions thus worked in favour of the German pilots as far as confirmed kills were concerned. Moreover, the authorities were still very adamant that confirmation by examination of wreckage or independent observers had to be considered before a confirmed kill would be awarded. In the case of the Russian Front, this often proved a lot easier than it did, for example, over England and, to a certain extent, France during the early 1940s, and helped to maintain the high victory scores credited to Luftwaffe pilots.

So, all the factors briefly outlined here must be taken into account when looking at individual scores, and for those who wish to pursue such lines of investigation some of the books listed in the Bibliography will prove rewarding. Finally, before moving on to take a short look at the careers of some of the pilots who achieved 'ace' status, let us see if there is an answer to another question.

WHAT MAKES
AN ACE?

*T*here are many answers to this question, most being based on how the individual reader wishes to interpret the many factors involved. To a great extent it is an unanswerable question, for it it is doubtful if many common factors would be discovered if every ace was studied in great depth. But perhaps there is one factor, and that might well be 'opportunity'.

However good a flyer, however good a marksman, however good his tactical awareness, a pilot could only benefit from those qualities given the right opportunity. Many exceptionally gifted pilots were never in the right place at the right time, so never had the chance to shine in combat. Similarly many men who were only average, or perhaps even below average, had many opportunities to meet the enemy; many failed because of their shortcomings, but some clearly succeeded. These may appear to be rather obvious statements, but they are so often overlooked when reading accounts of those who did achieve a degree of immortality. Let us consider a couple of examples.

In the early days of the Second World War, many RAF pilots flew in France using old-fashioned tactics which cost quite a few of them their lives. Later, on returning to England with a few victories recorded, they were 'rested' during the Battle of Britain so were denied the opportunity to increase their scores. Later, as the flow of pilots increased, those coming from training schools with above-average assessments were often trained as instructors, and were thus denied the opportunity many of their apparently less able companions were given when they reached their squadrons.

Decisions taken at all levels can also have far reaching results. Wing Commander 'Bunny' Stone was a pre-war Cranwell-trained pilot who achieved four victories with No 3 Squadron in France in 1940, and a further three in the Far East, including the first Japanese bomber to be shot down over Rangoon at night. In an interview, he recounted that when he was CO of No 17 Squadron he was ordered to take three Hurricanes deep into Japanese-held territory to strafe an airfield. He pointed out that even with long-range tanks the Hurricanes would only just have enough fuel to complete the round trip, even providing the pilots' dead reckoning navigation was spot on, but he was still told to carry out the mission. Eventually he agreed only on condition that he personally selected the other two pilots, and when told he could do so he named them. Later on, the sortie was cancelled since the authorities realized that if the Hurricanes failed to return they would have lost the three most experienced pilots then in the Far East. One of the three was Sqn Ldr Frank Carey who was to become arguably one of the greatest RAF Second World War aces. So here is an example of a situation that could have led to the deaths of at least two men who later achieved 'ace' status. Stone later went on to command No 135 Squadron in India, but his career never flourished after his promising early start and he still claims that this is mainly as a result of the stand against authority he took in Burma, which gave Frank Carey the opportunity to go on to find fame.

There must be countless other examples in every air force in which we must form our own conclusions as to what makes an ace, or at least what is the major contributory factor.

Any ace did, of course, rely on strong support and vigilance from his wing man, and many of those who survived combat are only too ready to acknowledge this. Sometimes the two formed a team and flew regularly together, but there are an equal number of examples indicating that the same man did not always fly on an ace's wing. This again is a fascinating subject that opens a whole new area of exploration for those who might be tempted into studying the subject in greater depth after reading this 'appetizer'. It must be remembered that although at a conservative estimate ace pilots and crews probably accounted for over 50 per cent of the total aerial claims made, they were only the sharply-honed edge of a sword and could not have operated without the strength of the blade in support.

It has been estimated that during the Second World War over 2,200 British, Commonwealth and American pilots, a similar number of Russians, and perhaps at least 4,000 Germans, obtained five aerial victories. Add to these those of the First War, other theatres, and post-war combats, and the final total is considerable. The fifty selected here have nothing particular in common other than at least the mandatory five kills, and perhaps that crucial opportunity of having been in the right place at the right time to get them. I have attempted to select those who came from widely different backgrounds, followed many varied paths before becoming fighter pilots, and had a wide range of temperaments and educational and social upbringings. Some have slipped into obscurity, others are still recalled with admiration, affection or even notoriety.

One aim had been to show that the steely-eyed, lantern-jawed hero of popular fiction was very much in the minority— if in reality he ever existed. In some cases complete books have been devoted to the chosen subject, while others will be new to the reader, so the selection must be regarded as an appetizer. If it proves a sufficient appetizer for the reader to go on to sample a comprehensive main course, it will have fulfilled a mission which can be summed up by the three letters 'DCO' which were often entered in the Flight Authorisation Book after a sortie: 'Duty Carried Out'.

THE RULES OF
AIR FIGHTING

*I*t seems odd to speak of rules when men were hell-bent on killing each other and survival was the name of the game, but there was,
always has been, and no doubt always will be a comradeship
and chivalry among those who fly. True enough, there are many accounts,
especially from First World War diaries and letters, of pilots deliberately
aiming at the men in the machines rather than the vulnerable parts of the
aircraft. Many of these are of course true, but some are tinged with
over-zealous drama aimed at impressing those at home. There are also some
accounts of pilots going to great lengths and personal danger to
save the lives of those with thom they had been engaged in mortal combat
a few moments before. But overall, most pilots viewed the combats
as straight encounters between men and machines, and to prove the
comradeship of airmen there are many accounts of those who were vanquished and fell into enemy territory being fêted and entertained by their
opposite numbers until such time as they were whisked off into
captivity.

'Beware of the Hun in the sun' was one of the catch-phrases of First
World War combat which still equally applied in the Second War. In
today's missile age, when sophisticated electronic devices warn aircrew that
an enemy has them locked on radar and a tone warns that a missile has been
fired, many might feel that the 'mark one eyeball' is obsolete. But as
recently as 1987, a pilot who had seen jet combat in Vietnam told the author
that there was still some adherence to the ten rules of air fighting first
published by Adolf 'Sailor' Malan in 1940. These were widely circulated in
Fighter Command and were also seen during the first days of jet fighter
combat in Korea. The same pilot added, 'When conditions are favourable
and you switch off all the modern electronic gadgets, it is still very much a
fighter pilot's world; you can creep up on an adversary and the first he
knows about it is when 30 mm cannon shells start taking pieces out of his
aircraft. Believe me, that really gets the adrenalin flowing and shows that
the good old-fashioned cannon shell can be just as effective as an electroni-
cally aimed missile homing on heat or what have you.'

Malan's ten rules of air fighting, which still form a part of the fighter
pilot's bible, are as follows:

1 Wait until you see the whites of his eyes. Fire short bursts of one to two seconds, and only when your sights are definitely 'on'.

2 Whilst shooting, think of nothing else. Brace the whole of the body, have both hands on the stick, concentrate on your ring sight.

3 Always keep a sharp look-out. 'Keep your finger out'.

4 Height gives you the initiative.

5 Always turn and face the attack.

6 Make your decisions promptly. It is better to act quickly even though your tactics are not of the best.

7 Never fly straight and level for more than thirty seconds in the combat area.

8 When diving to attack, always leave a proportion of your formation above to act as top guard.

9 INITIATIVE, AGGRESSION, AIR DISCIPLINE, AND TEAM-WORK are words that MEAN something in air fighting.

10 Go in quickly—Punch hard—Get out!

Obviously some of the rules have now been overtaken by modern control systems and sighting equipment, but many of them still ring true and make good common sense. Malan clearly based some of his thoughts on the dictum originally penned by the First World War ace Oswald Boelcke, who many still consider to be the greatest example of what a fighter pilot should be. And he is just one of the parade of fifty aces who fill the following pages, an undoubtedly brilliant strategist, organizer and fighter pilot who was responsible for laying the guide lines followed by the Imperial German Air Force and its fighter pilots in the first days of aerial conflict.

THE FIRST WORLD WAR ACES

ALBERT BALL

(RFC)

*L*ike many of the 'aces' of the early war period, Albert Ball was very much a loner; there are probably many reasons for this, not the least being that he was very introverted, probably stemming from nothing more sinister than his extreme youth. In analysing any event or personality from a distance, it is easy to arrive at many conclusions, and there are those who have chosen to read into Ball's character a sinister side associated with his devotion to his mother. The fact that he clearly had a deep affection for her is no different from many young men of the period who went more or less straight from a boarding or public school into the army. Such men had the self-assurance of depending on their own confidence, but on the other hand many had little or no experience of life away from the home environment.

It is not too surprising, therefore, that Ball wrote frequently to his mother, who responded with love and tenderness and often sent him parcels of his favourite treats in the same way that any parent would, and the same way that she had when he was at school. The important thing to remember is that Ball was an 18-year-old when he enlisted into the British Army in October 1914, and was gazetted as a 2nd Lieutenant with the Sherwood Foresters; he had not reached his majority and was still basically a shy young officer when he met his death on 7 May 1917.

It would be easy to claim that Ball's 'killer instinct', if indeed it even existed, was cultivated on the playing fields of his public school; such an upbringing, where no quarter was asked or given, certainly contributed, but his ability is more likely attributable to his lightning reactions, his sharp eye and his almost perfect co-ordination. Ball had always been interested in things mechanical and, like many of his contemporaries, the aeroplane had a strong enough fascination for him to pay for his own flying lessons at Hendon.

At almost the same time as he was commissioned, he gained his Royal Aero Club certificate. In January 1916 he received his RFC wings and the following month joined No 13 Sqn in France, flying BE 2cs. He also flew the squadron's single-seater Bristol Scout, and longed for the time when he could fly such aircraft regularly instead of the cumbersome reconnaissance machines. His chance came with No 11 Sqn in May, but although he had several encounters with the enemy and no doubt was responsible for causing some to crash, his official first victory did not come until 2 July when he engaged a Roland C 11 and its crash was confirmed by ground observers.

Ball had trimmed his Nieuport to be tail heavy, thus freeing both his hands from the control stick when he needed to rearm the wing-mounted Lewis gun; he also perfected a technique whereby he could aim and handle the gun better with both hands instead of having to fly with one and manage the firing with the other. His normal method of attack was to approach his quarry from beneath, pull the Lewis gun into a vertical position and empty at least three-quarters of a drum of ammunition into the underside of the enemy aircraft, a technique not too far removed from the vertical-firing Schräge Musik cannons of the Luftwaffe night fighters in the Second War.

At the end of July, Ball was awarded the MC and after some home leave was posted back to No 8 Sqn flying two-seaters. He saw this as a warning that his award may have made him appear conceited, but rather than complain too loudly he set about using his BE 2d in an offensive role, much to the consternation of his gunner/observer. Following the destruction of an observation balloon by the simple expedient of dropping bombs on it, the hierarchy got the message and he was returned to single-seaters with No 11 Sqn in August 1916, heralding the start of an impressive run of success.

Ball preferred to operate alone and devised a method whereby he took the enemy formations by storm. Approaching from the *front*, he dived into their midst causing them to scatter in all directions, then turned, selected a victim and carried out his proven underside attack. His total of confirmed kills during this period was not as high as many believe, but he was certainly a thorn in the side of enemy reconnaissance squadrons, forcing many to abandon their briefed tasks and force land, so his contribution was just as effective as those who revelled in sending aircraft after aircraft to a flaming end.

Ball returned to England at the end of 1916 and was fêted by the popular press; he carried out several tours of aircraft factories, but much preferred the comparative solitude of a squadron mess. By this time, he had been awarded the DSO and Bar as well as the Russian Order of St George. At last he managed to get out of the limelight and return to France where he joined No 56 Sqn flying SE 5s, although he retained his favourite Nieuport scout with its distinctive red spinner. He had several encounters with the infamous 'Flying Circus' and on 6 May claimed his last victim when he despatched Vizfeldwebel Jaeger of *Jagdstaffel* (fighter squadron) 20, on this occasion flying the Nieuport.

On the evening of the 7 May, he led an escort patrol to cover No 70 Sqn's Sopwith 1½ Strutters, but the formation was ambushed by *JG* 1; in the confused fighting, several SE 5s were shot down. Ball failed to return and was later found dead in his smashed aircraft. For a short period his demise was attributed to Lothar von Richthofen, but this claim was not substantiated as neither the SE nor Ball had been hit by machine-gun fire. It is believed that he became disorientated in cloud and was unable to regain control of his aircraft.

On 21 July 1917, his proud parents travelled from their home in Nottingham—Ball's birthplace—to receive from the hands of King George V the posthumously awarded Victoria Cross. His final tally was 44, comprising 21 shot down, one balloon, one shared victory, and 20 forced to land.

WILLIAM BARKER

(RFC)

*T*o the men of the Highland Light Infantry, the sound of aerial combat was not so unusual. But on 27 October 1918, when they heard the chattering of machine-guns and looked towards the sky, they were shocked to see a lone Sopwith Snipe twisting and turning to evade the attention of a whole *Jagdeschwader* (fighter wing) of Fokker D VIIs. As the Snipe fought against the 60 German aircraft, it occasionally spun seemingly out of control, would then recover, shoot at its antagonists once again, then fall into a stomach-wrenching spin. Eventually it spun almost to the ground before levelling off, skimming some trees then hitting the ground at about 90 mph, tearing off its undercarriage and shedding debris before finally coming to rest some 200 yards from the initial impact point.

The infantrymen rushed to the wreck and found the pilot unconscious in his blood-spattered cockpit. The Snipe (*E8102*) had been hit over 300 times, the pilot's legs had been shattered by machine-gun bullets and were attached by sinew alone, his left arm hung uselessly with the elbow seriously injured, and his face was covered with blood from a broken nose (incidentally, the only injury received in the crash). Lifting the pilot from the remains of his aircraft, the battle-hardened soldiers thought it only a question of time before he became another grim statistic. Taken to a hospital in Rouen, he lay unconscious for ten days before recovering to learn that he had shot down four aircraft in the space of his last 40-minute combat, and had been awarded the Victoria Cross.

Major William George Barker was a Canadian who had travelled from his native country in 1915 to fight in the trenches. On that fateful day in October 1918, he had been returning to England to take command of the school of air fighting at Hounslow when he had seen a lone Rumpler and not been able to resist the temptation of adding just one more victory to his credit. He had done this successfully, first killing the gunner then watching the pilot parachute to safety, but, like so many other aces, he had made the fatal error of not heeding his own advice, and had not seen the four *Jastas* (2, 26, 27 and 36) of *JG* 3 stepped up from ground level to 20,000 feet.

In the first encounter his Snipe had been hit several times and his right leg smashed by an incendiary bullet; this had brought about the first spin seen from the ground. He had recovered at 6,000 feet only to be rendered unconscious by another wound which had brought another spin, but once more the slipstream and unfamiliar motion of the aircraft had brought him back to reality and once again he had fought off the enemy scouts until another wound had made him pass out yet again. This time he had recovered at a very low level and had attempted the crash landing which he miraculously survived.

His tenacity was such that he recovered the full use of his limbs and was able to attend the investiture at which he received his VC from King George V. He was one of those men who could be termed a natural survivor. Born in Manitoba on 3 November 1894, he went to France in 1915 and survived the infamous first use of gas by the Germans at Ypres before, like many who had followed a similar path, transferring to the RFC. He served as an air mechanic and gunner on BE 2s with No 9 Squadron, was commissioned as an observer in April 1916 and served with No 4 Sqn on the Somme. Later he was accepted for pilot training, and his outstanding natural aptitude was soon evident when he flew solo after only 55 minutes; in January 1917 he received the coveted 'wings'.

His first combat experience as a pilot came on 25 March 1917 in the unwieldy RE 8 (the 'Harry Tait' as it was known to the RFC) when he shot down a reconnaissance aircraft to add to his score as a gunner/observer. Soon afterwards, he survived a crash-landing when his seriously damaged RE nosed over as he attempted to put it down. He returned to England and converted to the Sopwith Camel, with which he immediately fell in love, and on his return to the Western Front soon demonstrated the virtues of this most famous of all First World War aircraft with two victories in one combat.

By October, his score stood at 5 when, with No 28 Sqn, he was moved to Northern Italy as part of the British Expeditionary Force. The RFC squadrons were soon in action in support of the Italians and naturally Barker was in the forefront. On 29 November 1917, flying Camel *B6313*, he recorded the first British victory on the Italian Front. Although not the greatest exponent of the Camel, he earned the accolade of 'the artist with a pair of Vickers', for his marksmanship was exceptional. Victories mounted very quickly, as did other adventures which included flying a Caproni bomber to drop an Italian spy by parachute behind the Austrian lines. His score was marked on his aircraft by white stripes painted on the fuselage, and between April and July he accounted for 16 enemy aircraft.

Promoted to Major in July 1918, he took command of No 139 Sqn equipped with Bristol Fighters. He desperately wanted to take his Camel, but this was forbidden by the authorities. However, he overcame this by having it returned to a central depot for maintenance from where he arranged its temporary attachment to No 139 Sqn. Later, with the war in Italy virtually over, he was recalled to England, but persuaded his chiefs that he must have a further tour on the Western Front if he was to be able to teach efficiently the tactics of air fighting in the modern aircraft then being used, and encountered, by the RAF. This request was granted, and in

September 1918 he reported to No 201 Sqn where he was assigned a brand new Snipe. Just fifteen days before the Armistice, he said his farewells, climbed aboard his aircraft and headed towards England. At 20,000 feet over the Forêt de Mormal, he had spotted a Rumpler CVII and had not been able to resist that one last tilt at the enemy . . .

Barker's final tally was 52, and in addition to the VC he was also awarded a DSO and Bar, MC and two Bars, the *Croix de Guerre* and the Italian *Valore Militare*. His luck finally ran out on 12 March 1930, when he was killed in a flying accident in Canada.

RAYMOND COLLISHAW

(RFC)

*L*t Karl Allmenroeder, the 22-year-old deputy commander of von Richt-hofen's famous *Jasta* 11, peered anxiously over the white-painted cowling of his Albatross D 111; glancing to his left he saw the signal from his wingman, indicating that the British Sopwith Triplanes had fallen for the trap. A smile creased his face as he thought how simple it had been, how soon the *Jasta* would prove which aircraft was superior. It was 27 June 1917, and two days earlier Allmenroeder, who had been awarded the 'Blue Max' on the 17th of the month, had encountered the legendary Triplanes for the first time and had managed to destroy one of the famous five black-cowled versions, *Black Sheep*, flown by Flt Sub-Lt J. E. Nash, before having to use the superior speed of the Albatross to escape.

This brief encounter had shown the German pilots that the stories they had heard about the Triplane were true, that it was extremely manoeuvr-able and could 'turn on a sixpence', getting out of a seemingly impossible situation with ease. For two days the *Jasta* had pondered tactics, eventually deciding to split into high and low formations, the low acting as the bait; when the Triplanes dived on them, the higher element would use their better diving speed to teach the British pilots a lesson they would not forget. It was a good plan, but it backfired when the top flight failed to spot the attacking Triplanes until it was far too late. As the Germans tried to out-turn the British aircraft, the Albatross with the white cowling and elevators was cut off. A black-cowled Triplane made one firing pass and the German biplane was seen to glide slowly earthwards; the angle steepened and the aircraft plunged into the ground on the outskirts of Lille. Von Richthofen's deputy had met his end at the hands of the most outstanding RNAS pilot of the war, Raymond Collishaw, flying his equally famous Triplane *Black Maria*.

Collishaw was a Canadian born in British Columbia, and had enlisted in the Canadian Merchant Marine whilst he was still in his teens. At eighteen, he sailed on Scott's Antartic expedition and in 1914, when war broke out in Europe, he still had a taste for adventure so quit the Fishery Protection Service and at his own expense travelled to England where he enlisted in the Royal Naval Air Service. Qualifying as a pilot in early 1916, his first assignment was to No 3 Wing at Luxeil-les-Bains flying Sopwith 1½

Strutters.

In October, he recorded his first three victories and the following February moved to No 3 (Naval) Squadron under the command of fellow Canadian R. H. Mulock. His prowesss was soon evident when he shot down an Albatross D 111 in March. By now, the Canadian's ability had been recognized and it was no surprise when he became the commander of 'B' Flight of No 10 (Naval) Squadron based at Furnes. It was now that he selected four other Canadians to form the nucleus of what became known as 'Naval Ten', five men flying five Sopwith Triplanes all with black-painted cowlings and carrying the names *Black Maria, Black Death, Black Sheep, Black Roger* and *Black Prince.*

Whilst the RFC was being cut to pieces in the Arras area, the RNAS squadrons enjoyed aerial superiority over Dunkirk and were keeping the sea approaches open. Collishaw's score mounted by leaps and bounds, recording four victories in the first 12 days of May. At the beginning of June, No 10(N) Sqn was moved to Droglandt under the auspices of No 11 Wing RFC, and soon the black-cowled Triplanes were making their presence felt with Collishaw leading by example and shooting down four German aircraft in five days. On 6 June, he accounted for three in one action and was subsequently awarded a deserved DSC; by the 15th of the month his overall total stood at 23. The action of 27 June was the prelude to a sustained period in which the naval Triplanes continually mauled the Germans, and on one occasion, 6 July, Collishaw came very close to an encounter with von Richthofen, when RNAS aircraft encountered some FE 2s fighting from a defensive circle against a formidable array of Albatrosses. The gunner of one FE (2nd Lt A. E. Woodbridge) hit von Richthofen's aircraft, forcing the 'Red Baron' into an emergency landing before the two great aces could clash (see page 52).

With his score at 28, Collishaw returned to Canada for a rest, but in November 1917 was back in action taking command of No 13(N) Sqn flying the most famous fighter of the First World War, the redoubtable Sopwith Camel. The following January he moved to No 3(N) Sqn which, on 1 April 1918, became No 203 Sqn Royal Air Force. His mastery of the Camel was as good as that of the Triplane, and by the end of the war he was undefeated with 62 confirmed victories to his name.

In a further century of combats he may well have accounted for 15 more enemy aircraft but these could not be confirmed. His exploits earned him a DSO and Bar, and a Bar to his DSC, and it is somewhat surprising that he did not receive the ultimate accolade of a Victoria Cross. Continuing to serve after the war, he commanded No 47 Sqn in Southern Russia where he scored at least two more victories in support of General Denekin's campaign against the Red Army. He eventually rose to the rank of Air Vice Marshal and commanded the Western Desert Air Force in 1941–42.

LANOE HAWKER

(RFC)

*T*here is a tendancy to consider an ace's total score to be the ultimate criterion, and this can often lead to all other elements being forgotten. For instance, it is not often that the name of Major Lanoe Hawker VC will be found in any lists of First World War aces since his total of nine victories is well below the minimum adopted by the majority of chroniclers. His inclusion because he happens to be the first RFC 'ace' is also to a degree not that relevant, but because he was one of those pilots who had to learn from the very beginning and had a natural aptitude for flying that freed him to use his talents in developing tactics and, above all, to instil confidence in many young pilots, means that he must be rated as one of the great fighter pilots. There can be little doubt that his skill in aerobatics, his marksmanship and his timing, especially when flying against much more modern machines, were some of the attributes that enabled him to make his mark in the annals of the RFC. Hawker was one of the few men who can be truly described as a natural leader, and there is no doubt that but for his untimely death he would have risen to very high rank and authority.

Hawker, who came from a military background, was born on 30 December 1890 in Longparish, Hampshire, and at the age of eleven entered the Royal Naval College at Dartmouth to follow in the footsteps of his father who had served with honour in the senior service. Sadly, his ambition crumbled with ill health which forced him to leave the Navy, but the military was ingrained in him and such was his desire to serve King and country that he enlisted in the Royal Military Academy at Woolwich and was commissioned into the Royal Engineers on 20 July 1911. The previous June, he and his brother Tyrrel had become so taken by the new vogue of flying that they had joined the Royal Aero Club and started flying lessons at Hendon. Lanoe's work with the engineers meant that he made slow progress, but in March 1913 he finally obtained his pilot's certificate, numbered 435. His request for attachment to the RFC was granted in 1914, and he underwent military flying training at the Central Flying School, Upavon, graduating from 'D' Flight in October.

The same month, he embarked for France with No 6 Squadron and was soon flying over enemy lines, first as an observer then piloting his own BE

2a. Hawker had a naturally aggressive outlook and, in attempts to carry the fight to the enemy, often carried hand-grenades, darts and other missiles which he threw over the side of his aircraft into enemy positions. On his first solo sortie, he encountered an enemy reconnaissance machine which he instantly attacked despite the limiting factor of having only his service revolver as an offensive weapon. This sidearm had no affect on the enemy aircraft, but such was Hawker's determination that he resolved to increase his fire-power and promptly fitted a rifle to the BE 2c he was by now flying. The main objective of the squadron was to pin-point enemy artillery batteries and infantry movements, and Hawker quite frequently ignored the barrage of fire directed at his aircraft so that he could concentrate on reporting their positions accurately.

In fact, on many occasions he flew lower than prudence dictated to encourage the enemy to engage him so that he could pin-point their positions. On 18 April 1915, armed with only three 20 lb bombs plus an assortment of grenades, he set out to bomb the Zeppelin sheds at Gontrode near Ghent. Unknown to the RFC or the intrepid Lieutenant, the LZ 35 which was normaley resident had crashed five days earlier, but Hawker pressed home his attack despite accurate machine-gun fire from a tethered guard balloon, and scored a direct hit on what was unfortunately an empty hangar. This exploit earned him a deserved DSO and promotion to Captain, as well as to the command of the squadron.

On the 24th of the month, Lady Luck deserted him—whilst carrying out a low-level patrol, he was wounded in the left foot. Despite severe pain, he flew again two days later and, with Lt Wylie as his observer, drove off three German reconnaissance aircraft with the sole aid of a rifle. His injury was such that sick leave was inevitable, but after two weeks he returned and once again was in the thick of the fighting. It was about this time that with the help of the then Air Mechanic E. J. Elton, he contrived to fit a Lewis gun to a Bristol Scout; in the absence of any synchronization mechanism, the two men fixed the gun to fire at an angle, thus avoiding hitting the propellor. This meant, however, that he needed to attack any adversary in a crab-like approach. This was put to the test on 7 June when his fire sent a two-seater spinning earthwards; a similar action on 21 June brought inconclusive results, although the aircraft he attacked was seen to be emitting smoke as it descended.

The next day he survived a crash with minor injuries when he force landed the Bristol, but was soon in action again with another modified aircraft and on 25 July set out on an offensive patrol. To put into perspective the fighting spirit of Hawker, it must be remembered that his sorties in the Scout were flown in addition to his normal flying of recon-naissance patrols in an FE 2b. His skill was such that on the day in question he achieved three victories, the first being an Aviatik C type, the second another Aviatik and the third, and most difficult, an Albatross C1. The observer in the latter was Hauptmann Roser who hit back at the Bristol with his Parabellum and might well have caused the British pilot some problems had he not been thrown from his aircraft at 10,000 feet as it attempted to avoid the gunfire from the Bristol. Hawker's exploits on this July day, coupled with his determination during almost a year of continuous operational flying, earned him the award of the Victoria Cross which was gazetted on 24 August.

His continuing success with the Bristol and his outstanding and aggressive leadership eventually led to his appointment to command No 24 Squadron, the first British single-seater fighter squadron. Taking up his appointment on 25 September 1915, Hawker had to wait until January 1916 before the squadron's first DH 2 aircraft arrived. With no experienced pilots to help, he carried the full burden of training his protégés, and at all times drummed into them his basic philosophy of 'attack everything', two words that were eventually to appear on the operational notice board. With the 25-year-old Major Hawker in command, the squadron arrived in France on 7 February and started working up with patrols north of the Somme.

It was not long before the Fokker Eindecker was encountered and the pusher biplane with its forward-firing gun proved a match for the German monoplane which had hitherto struck fear into RFC reconnaissance crews. At that time, squadron commanders were officially forbidden to fly on combat patrols, but Hawker quite rightly thought this to be a rather stupid dictum and overcame it by leaving his name off operational orders and flying as a member of the flight subordinate to the Flight Commander. The squadron achieved a growing reputation, and by November had recorded 70 victories, with Hawker's personal tally standing at nine, although it seems likely that this may well have been higher.

With over a year at the helm behind him, Hawker knew that his days with No 24 were numbered; he had already been told unofficially that he would soon be promoted to command a wing. The afternoon of 23 November 1916 saw him listed as No 2 to 'A' Flight's commander, Capt J. Andrews, in a four aircraft flight that included Lt Saundby (later to become Air Marshal Sir Robert Saundby) and Lt Crutch flying in the 'box'. Crutch was soon forced to abandon the patrol due to engine trouble but the other three pressed on. Spotting two reconnaissance aircraft, the leader led the British scouts into a diving attack, but as the Germans dived eastwards, Andrews suspected a trap and, looking up, spotted some Albatross D 2s circling and waiting for a chance to 'bounce' the unwary British pilots. Andrews and Saundby immediately broke off the pursuit of the two-seaters which had been the bait in the trap, but Hawker continued his relentless pursuit. By the time the two British pilots realised that their commander was not with them and turned back to help, three Albatrosses flown by members of *Jasta* 2 led by Lt Manfred von Richthofen were upon them.

Andrews' DH 2 was hit almost immediately and he turned back towards the British lines with an Albatross on his tail; Saundby managed to shoot down his Flight Commander's antagonist and escort him to a friendly airfield before returning to look for Hawker. Neither British pilot saw his squadron commander again. It is now known that with his line of retreat cut off, Hawker turned to face von Richthofen and for the next 35 minutes the two men were engaged in an aerial ballet in which neither held the upper hand long enough to deal a mortal blow to the other. The odds, however, were against Hawker—his aircraft was dated when compared with the Albatross, whose German pilot knew that sooner or later the British flyer would have to make a break for his own lines.

By skilful flying, Hawker edged the DH 2 closer and closer to safety, but with petrol running low was eventually forced to make a decision. He threw the aircraft into a loop to distract the German, and as he pulled out pushed the stick fully forward and dived at some speed towards safety. Von Richthofen also had problems; fuel and ammunition were getting low and he had already fired over 900 rounds at the DH 2 without any apparent success. But now, as the two machines screamed across the countryside at tree-top height, with the British pilot fish-tailing in an attempt to confuse the German's aim, he had one more chance. From a range of about 100 yards he tried a deflection shot as the DH 2 momentarily turned across him. The British aircraft staggered, then plunged to earth close to Luisenhof Farm, two miles south of Bapaume on the road to Flers.

The cellars of the farm were being used by a group of German Grenadiers commanded by Major von Schoenberg. They reached the downed British aircraft to find its pilot dead with just one bullet wound to the head, and this after 35 minutes of sustained aerial combat with a man who was destined to become Germany's best-known ace. Hawker, who was the 'Red Baron's' eleventh victim, was buried with full military honours alongside the wreckage of his aircraft.

Right *Major W. G. Barker VC* (Public Archives of Canada).

Below *Major W. G. Barker VC DSO MC with a Camel (B6313) shortly after his appointment to command No 139 Sqn. Note the 'red devil' mascot at the muzzle end of the guns. (via Chaz Bowyer).*

Left *Captain Albert Ball DSO MC (later VC) in front of his Nieuport Scout with No 60 Sqn RFC, September 1916* (Chaz Bowyer).

Below left *Major Raymond Collishaw DSO DSC DFC* (Chaz Bowyer).

Below *Major Lanoe Hawker VC DSO on 5 October 1915* (Chaz Bowyer).

Above *Major Edward Mannock VC DSO MC, of Nos 40, 74 and 85 Sqns, killed in action 26 July 1918. This picture was taken during training at Hendon in 1916-17 (Chaz Bowyer).*

Above right *Capt Georges Guynemer, the French ace who was killed in action on 11 September 1917 (Chaz Bowyer).*

Right *Rittmeister Manfred Freiherr von Richthofen in an Albatros DV cockpit, 1917 (Chaz Bowyer).*

Left *Hauptmann Oswald Boelcke who on 21 May 1916 at the age of 25 became the youngest man ever to hold the rank of Hauptmann in the Royal Prussian Army* (via Chaz Bowyer).

Below *Boelcke in the cockpit of a Fokker E 1* (Author's collection).

JAMES McCUDDEN

(RFC)

*A*uxi-le-Chateau, France, 9 July 1918. A single SE 5a taxies to the end of the field, turns into the wind, the engine idling as the pilot carries out his final checks. Then the leather-helmeted figure lifts his head from the cockpit, waves to a group of onlookers, and, checking all is clear behind, opens the throttle and starts his take-off run. The biplane gathers speed as it bounces across the field, until daylight appears beneath the wheels as its wings gather sufficient lift to carry it into the air. Suddenly the engine stutters, then stops; the horrified onlookers see the aircraft start to turn back towards the airfield, a natural but forbidden manoeuvre that pilots are taught to avoid from almost the first day of their flying training. The SE 5 loses speed, sideslips and ploughs into the ground with fatal results.

Another novice who had not digested the basic technique of engine failure on take-off? No, the pilot who met his death in this careless and unnecessary way was the newly promoted Major James Byford Thomas McCudden, who was setting out to take command of No 60 Squadron.

McCudden was not only a very experienced fighter pilot and ace with 57 victories, a Victoria Cross, two DSOs and two Military Crosses, but had also served as a flying instructor, which makes his attempt at a manoeuvre, the futility of which he must have drummed into pupils' ears on many occasions, even harder to understand. Like so many experienced pilots, it would seem that he had become overconfident, although perhaps unaware of it, and had gone against the rules that he should have had ingrained into his soul.

In April, at the age of 22, McCudden had become the most decorated member of the RFC or RNAS, and like Mick Mannock had risen from the ranks to become a senior officer. This was no mean accomplishment in the days when tradition and family background were vital ingredients to such elevated heights. Born on 25 March 1895, he had enlisted as a boy bugler in the Royal Engineers at the age of 15. In 1913 he had transferred to the RFC and become an air mechanic with No 3 Squadron, going to France with the unit in 1914 when war was declared. It was not too long before the young McCudden was flying as an observer in Farmans and in between operational flights managed to log some dual instruction on a Morane Parasol.

It was as a sergeant observer in December 1915 that he experienced his first taste of combat, and the following month received the *Croix de Guerre*. The same month he returned to England, having been selected for pilot training, and in July returned to France as something of a rarity—a Flight Sergeant pilot—flying DH 2s with No 29 Squadron. A month after starting his operational career as a pilot, he recorded his first victory when he downed a two-seater reconnaissance aircraft over Gheluve, a significant start since he was to become something of a specialist in stalking and destroying such machines, 45 featuring in his 57 victories.

His first decoration, the Military Medal, came on 1 October, and on the first day of 1917 he received his commission, a proud landmark for the young man from Gillingham.

He converted to Sopwith Pups and carried out a short spell as an instructor before serving briefly with No 66 Squadron. During this period, he flew a patrol with No 56 Squadron in an SE 5 and his prowess was noted by the squadron commander who requested that the by then Captain McCudden should join his squadron as a Flight Commander. Like many other pilots, McCudden developed a strong liking for the SE which he claimed was fast and comfortable; also, like many of his contemporaries, and probably because of his background, he could often be found tinkering with the aircraft's engine and machine-guns. In his quest to squeeze every ounce of performance from his mount, he fitted the streamlined spinner from a LVG to his favourite SE 5 (*A4891*). Although he expressed a strong liking for the Vickers-built SE 5 rather than the Royal Aircraft Factory's offering, it was in one of the latter aircraft (*A4763*) that he had the classic encounter with Werner Voss on 23 September 1917. Although he studied the tactics of the two-seater German aircraft and developed his own counter-tactics which brought him the majority of his victims, he could more than hold his own in a fighter-to-fighter situation. On two occasions he accounted for four German aircraft in one day, and his last triumph came on 16 February when he shot down a Hannover CL 111. He returned to England on 5 March and undertook another instructional tour before being promoted to Major and posted back to France.

In the last four months of his life he must have stressed the basic rules of flying to embryo pilots countless times; it is ironic indeed that he failed to heed his own instructions when it mattered most.

MICK MANNOCK

(RFC)

*T*he fascination of First World War aviation and aces is still probably higher than that of any other period, and as long as historians
and enthusiasts debate this conflict there will always be controversy as to
who was the greatest ace. This is, of course, an impossible question to
answer, as so many contradictory and contributing factors must be taken
into account. But whatever parameters are used, Edward 'Mick' Mannock
will always be near the top, and in most cases will emerge as *the*
British ace.

Mannock had an unusual start to his career when, as a telephone
engineer working in Turkey in 1914, he was interned on the declaration of
war but was later released since the Turks felt that defective vision in his
right eye would render him non-combatant. Their mistake is understand-
able but was a costly one to at least 73 German pilots. Like many aces,
Mannock's total score is uncertain, but as far as this work is concerned, that
is of little relevance.

In today's world, Mannock would no doubt be considered an 'angry
young man'—he was the complete opposite of, for example, Lanoe Hawker, who came from a moneyed family and had been brought up with all the
so-called trappings of an upper class background. Born into a working class
family, Mannock seems to have grown up with a 'chip on his shoulder'; he
had little compassion for the enemy and was totally opposed to the so-called
chivalry of the air, shunning such activities as paying respect to the enemy,
dropping notes or wreaths over enemy airfields or even allowing downed
airmen to evacuate their machines. His character in this respect can be
illustrated by the comment he made on learning of the death of von
Richthofen—'I hope he roasted the whole way down'.

He was totally ruthless in battle, and this was typified by the occasion
when he badly damaged a two-seater reconnaissance aircraft, forcing it to
land, then continually strafed it until both crew members were dead.
However, there is very strong evidence to suggest that he was a born leader
and admired by his men for this quality, if not for some of what his
contemporaries considered to be ungentlemanly habits.

Mannock was attracted to the challenge of flying and managed to
conceal his defective vision well enough to be accepted for pilot training. He

joined No 40 Squadron flying Nieuports in France in April 1917, and claimed his first victory on 7 July 1917. Mannock was a slow starter, not due to any hesitancy but because he believed in learning every aspect of air fighting before taking chances. This accounts for the delay in the recording of his next victory which came in July and was followed in the following two months by 17 more, including the German ace Lt Joachim von Bertrab on 12 August.

Although having little compassion for the enemy, Mannock took a great deal of interest in the younger and less experienced pilots of his own squadron, shepherding and protecting them in combat situations, and helping them to gain confidence by letting them deal the final blow to aircraft that he himself had damaged and could well have claimed as victories. However, his ruthless streak often dominated his actions and there were some who obviously did not know him well who expressed horror on learning of the occasion in 1917, when his flight encountered a German training flight deep inside enemy airspace. Mannock dived on the instructor's lumbering Aviatik, then relentlessly pursued the five pupils in similar machines, dispatching each of them in turn to fiery ends.

Towards the end of 1917, he converted to the SE 5a and found that in this aircraft he had a superlative weapon that was a match for anything the enemy could put into the air. His first victory in this aircraft came on New Year's Day 1918, then he was posted home for a rest. Mannock returned to France in the spring of 1918 as a Flight Commander with the famous Tiger Squadron (No 74) which had formed at Northolt in July 1917, and whose motto 'I fear no man' could have been tailor-made for the one-eyed ace.

Mannock and his flight were soon in the thick of the fighting and his typically clinical approach was demonstrated to members of his unit when he engaged Lt Van Ira's Pflaz D 111. After trying to out-turn the SE 5 in the opening exchanges, the German opted to try a diving half-roll. Mannock followed and was quickly on the Pflaz's tail, firing as soon as he was in a good position.

The German pulled into a loop, still with the British aircraft close behind following every move as though they were performing formation aerobatics. By now, the German pilot must have realized that he had a master on his tail, so he tried spinning, but once again the SE 5 followed, firing at every opportunity but not recording many hits as the German pilot also handled his aircraft with skill. At 4,000 feet he abandoned the spin, and this gave Mannock the chance he had worked for; as the Pflaz levelled out and started trying to evade the fire from the British machine by twisting, Mannock laid off the right amount of deflection and administered what proved to be the *coup de grâce*.

In June 1918 he took over the command of No 85 Squadron from Billy Bishop, but just over a month later, on 26 July, he broke one of his own cardinal rules and allowed himself and another pilot to be lured into a trap by following a Junkers CL 1 which they had damaged. In the diving pursuit, Mannock's aircraft was hit, burst into flames and crashed.

Besides his final score being unknown, there is also doubt about the authenticity of some claims, but this is only because of the lack of supporting evidence. One of his biographers (Ira Jones, also an ace and former No 74 Squadron pilot) puts the total at 73, which seems too conveniently close to that of Bishop (72), whom Jones disliked. The citation to Mannock's Victoria Cross, gazetted after the war, quotes 50, but the true total of confirmed kills is now believed to be about 68.

Most of Mannock's victories were achieved over enemy territory, and unlike many other aces he was far from being a loner, preferring to lead his men from the front. It is probably these two important factors that would place him near, if not at, the top of any list of leading British aces. In addition to his Victoria Cross he was also awarded the DSO with two bars and the Military Cross with one bar.

GEORGES GUYNEMER

(FRENCH AIR FORCE)

*T*here are many occasions when the total score of an ace takes second place to his standing. Guynemer's total confirmed score, according to the system adopted by the French, was 54, which places him second to Réné Fonck, but in terms of popularity he is much better known than the leading French ace. Born in Paris on Christmas Eve 1894, the frail Frenchman, who was initially rejected on medical grounds for military service, was captivated by the aviation fever that swept through the country after Bleriot conquered the Channel. He was determined to become a pilot, and after his initial disappointment succeeded in bluffing his way, with the help of a few well-positioned friends, into the French Air Service as a mechanic.

It did not take him long to climb the next step, and early in 1915 he was accepted for pilot training making his first solo flight on 10 March. In June he joined *Escadrille* MS 3, and on 19 July manoeuvred his Morane Parasol into a position that enabled his observer to shoot down an Aviatik. He then moved to single-seater scouts starting with the Morane type N and then the Nieuport. Although he was shot down in September he was already being acclaimed a national hero as aerial victories in 1915 were fairly unusual. His conquest of the Aviatik brought him the *Medaille Militaire* on 4 August, this being the first of many decorations bestowed on him by a grateful country. On 8 December, he recorded his second confirmed kill, this time a LVG, and on the 14th another two-seater fell to his guns. On his 21st birthday, he received the Cross of the Legion of Honour, and was already being looked upon as invincible.

In February, the Battle of Verdun started with a vengeance, but Guynemer, now commissioned, was wounded on his second sortie and took no further part. Fit again for the Somme, he soon proved that he had lost none of his skills and by the end of July his score stood at 11. He liked to operate as a loner and perfected a method of attacking head-on which brought him incredible successes, especially when he started flying the SPAD S VII in July 1916. With this new aircraft, to which he had transferred the name *Vieux Charles* from his beloved Nieuport, his kill rate rose dramatically. On 23 September 1916 he shot down three Fokkers in a five-minute spell, was then hit by French artillery and actually crashed to the ground before his third victim! He was to survive five further crashes and also recorded several multiple victories.

The French authorities pressed him to rest as his failing health proved that the original medical rejection had probably been right. However, he felt that his place was in the front line fighting for France, telling his father that 'if one has not given everything one has given nothing'. On the morning of 11 September 1917, he took off from St Pol accompanied by Sous-Lieutnant Bozon-Verduraz, engaged an enemy two-seater but did not see the protective flight of Albatrosses above. The Frenchmen became separated and Guynemer was not seen again. The Germans claimed he was shot down by Lt Kurt Wissemann, and he and his aircraft were totally destroyed by an artillery barrage, but whatever happened the French ace had not survived his eighth crash.

His final score was 54, but had all his claims been allowed it would have been over 80. French schoolchildren were taught that the nation's hero had flown so high he could not come down again, a fitting end to the story of a man who certainly reached the highest pinnacles of success in every aspect of aerial fighting.

RAOUL LUFBERY

(FRENCH AIR FORCE)

*F*ire in the air is an element feared by all airmen. Even today, with modern in-flight extinguishers, heat detectors and warnings, it is still very bad news. Many First World War airmen feared it more than any other danger they were likely to encounter, some even vowing that in the event of their aircraft catching fire at a height which prevented them reaching the safety of the ground, they would use their service revolvers to bring a short sharp end to their life rather than a slow painful one by an ordeal of flame. In the absence of parachutes they had little chance of survival, the main hope being to push the stick forward and apply full rudder in the direction opposite to the prevailing fire; this would sideslip the aircraft and hopefully extinguish the flames or at least keep them at bay whilst some form of landing was attempted.

On Sunday 19 May 1918 near Nancy, a lone Nieuport 28 was stalking a German two-seater reconnaissance machine when the fighter pilot saw his chance, and with guns blazing raked the two-seater. The German observer managed to fire back, then witnesses on the ground heard the chatter of the Nieuport's guns cease and saw the aircraft turn away. It seemed as though the pilot was trying to clear a stoppage, then a small flicker of flame was seen. The pilot tried sideslipping, but the flames increased; the horrified onlookers saw the pilot climb on to the rear fuselage decking from where he appeared to be trying to reach back into the cockpit to control the now well-alight machine. With the flames getting a firm hold he had little chance, and suddenly threw himself off the doomed aircraft and crashed to his death into the village of Maron.

So died Gervais Raoul Lufbery, an American with a French-sounding name, fighting with a French squadron manned by American volunteers. His 17 victories placed him in joint fifth place as far as American pilots fighting in the First World War was concerned, but like Immelmann his name is remembered for a manoeuvre that was named after him: the defensive Lufbery circle. This manoeuvre, much favoured by Me 110 pilots in the Second War, involved flying in a defensive circle with each aircraft covering the one in front, much like a formation of covered waggons in the Wild West when under attack by marauding redskins. There is a good chance that this was, in fact, its origin, but the glamour of adding an ace's name to it was good for morale and the public image (it is doubtful if the pilot was even aware that his name was being used in this way). So, how did an American with a French name become a respected flyer and ace in what was primarily a European conflict?

Already 29 years old when the war started, Lufbery was over 30 before he qualified as a pilot, so in relative terms was well above the age of most aces, but became a typical schoolboy hero such as might have stepped straight from the pages of *Boys' Own*. Born to French parents on 14 March 1885, he emigrated with them to America in 1891. Always a boy with an adventurous and restless nature, he left home at 17 to seek his fortune and travelled through Europe to the Middle East, then back across America before arriving in the Philippines in 1908 as a member of the American Army.

In 1912, whilst in Saigon, he met the French adventurer Marc Pourpe who was introducing the outposts of the French Empire to the wonders of flying. Lufbery persuaded the Frenchman to take him on as a mechanic and thus was born a devotion to flying that was to take him back to the land of his birth to fight as an American in French uniform with a French fighter squadron staffed by fellow American adventurers. When war was declared, Pourpe immediately enlisted in the French air force, but, being a foreigner, Lufbery was not able to follow in his mentor's footsteps and was directed to the Foreign Legion. However, he was not a man to let a few regulations stand in his way, and within a few weeks was with *Escardrille* No 3 as Pourpe's mechanic.

In December 1914, Pourpe was killed and Lufbery applied, and was accepted, for pilot training. Seven months later he received his flying badge and in October 1915 was posted to *Escadrille de Bombardment* VB 106. Although he flew bombers for six months, his heart was really in the cut-and-thrust of the fighter squadrons, so he requested and obtained a transfer. The handling of bombers left a certain clumsiness, but he soon mastered this and on 24 May 1916 he joined *Escadrille Lafayette* where he flew his Nieuport with great deftness.

The *Lafayette* traced its origins to the *Escadrille Americaine* formed in April 1916 as a French fighter squadron commanded by French officers but with American pilots. At that time America was of course neutral, and pressure was put on diplomats to drop the American connection. As a result, the name *Lafayette* replaced the rather obvious American title. Of the original seven American pilots who formed the nucleus of the squadron, only three survived the war. One of them, Victor Chapman, was the first American to be killed in the conflict when he was shot down on 23 June 1916.

Two months after joining the squadron, Lufbery scored his first victory when he accounted for a two-seater on 31 July, following this three days later with a double victory over Fort Vaux. By October he had achieved 'ace' status, and by the end of 1916 his total stood at seven. Lufbery flew with the French squadron throughout 1917, converting to the famous SPAD Scout. His score steadily mounted, and had reached 17 confirmed victories by the end of 1917.

In January 1918, he was transferred to the newly formed American Air Service to instruct and advise the pilots of the 94th Aero Squadron; this meant a return to flying his beloved Nieuport, although he was forbidden by the American authorities to fly in combat. However, on 19 May he could not resist chasing a marauding enemy reconnaissance aircraft, and paid the ultimate penalty.

The top-scoring American ace with 22 victories is Captain Eddie Rickenbacker of the 94th Aero Squadron, but it is fellow American Major Raoul Lufbery who is revered in France as a national hero, an accolade that few who are not French nationals have ever achieved.

FRANCESCO BARACCA

(ITALIAN AIR FORCE)

*I*t is strange how nations who are quick to recognize the potential of new inventions and take an early initiative often seem to fall by the wayside with the passage of time. The Italians fit into this category as far as the aeroplane is concerned, for although as early as 1910 they had established the first military flying school and were the first to mount military operations using aircraft in Libya in 1911–2, they never managed to become leaders in the strategic and tactical use of air power.

However, it is not surprising that the typical Italian flair and penchant for all things mechanical produced some very fine aviators, among them being their leading First World War ace, Maggiore Francesco Baracca. In October 1907, the 19-year-old Italian, much against the wishes of his parents, entered the *Scula Militare,* emerging one year later with a commission in the Royal Piedmont Cavalry. Like many other flying aces, he soon changed the saddle of a horse for the cockpit of an aeroplane, and by 1912 was a qualified pilot. He missed the air fighting in Libya, however, and for the next three years toured Italian bases instructing in all aspects of aviation.

When his country finally entered the Great War, he was assigned to the 70 Squadriglia flying Nieuport II BeBes, and on 11 April 1916, after carefully stalking an Austrian Aviatik, he recorded his first victory when he forced the aircraft down using a technique he was often to employ, attacking from behind and below. Dogged by several gun stoppages when in advantageous positions, he had to wait until 16 May for further success, this time intercepting 14 Austrian bombers which were using cloud cover and the half-light of dawn to attack Italian positions. By 25 November 1916, he had achieved ace status and, to celebrate, painted a prancing horse on his aircraft, this becoming his personal emblem for the rest of his flying career.

In May 1917 he was one of several experienced pilots who formed the core of 91 Squadriglia equipped with the formidable French SPAD SVII, and on 6 June he assumed command of this unit which operated from the airfield at Istrana. Baracca's score mounted steadily, although on many occasions he was lucky to survive. For example, he narrowly escaped from a confrontation with Albatross D IIIs on 25 October when his aircraft was badly damaged by gunfire, but he ended that day with one victory from five encounters. Between September and November 1917, his score rose by 11, taking his overall total to 29, at which point the authorities sent him to Turin to advise Ansaldo on the development of a 'home-grown' fighter. After helping to lay the foundations for the SVA 5, he returned to the combat zone and was soon back in action re-opening his account with an Albatross D III on 3 May 1918, and four more during the last Austrian effort to cross the river frontier protecting Venice.

Baracca did not confine himself or his squadron to purely air-to-air combat. He could also see the importance of supporting ground troops by strafing, and on 19 June 1918 he mounted such an attack on enemy trenches at Montello. The three SPADS were seen operating at a very low level, but on return to Treviso Baracco was missing. His wrecked aircraft was later found by Italian troops on the banks of the Piave, the ace still in his cockpit with one fatal bullet wound to the head. As is the case of von Richthofen, it has never been conclusively proved whether this wound came from another aircraft or from ground fire, but it is strongly believed that credit for shooting down Italy's 34-victory top-scoring pilot goes to the gunner of an Austrian two-seater.

Baracca is still remembered today in a manner of which he would have heartily approved. After the war, his mother gave the prancing horse symbol, painted on his aircraft, to a young racing driver, Enzo Ferrari, who founded the famous company bearing his name and whose cars still carry the First World War ace's battle emblem to every corner of the world.

OSWALD BOELCKE

(IMPERIAL GERMAN AIR FORCE)

*B*orn on 9 May 1891 in Saxony, Boelcke was the third of six children, and to his father, a former rector of a Lutheran School in Buenos Aires, he seemed the least likely to be interested in a military career. Oswald spent a lot of time reading, and seemed to be destined for an academic career, but to his family's surprise the Kaiser's army proved to be a greater attraction than architecture which at one time looked to be the young man's forte. In March 1911, he duly reported to the Cadet Academy at Koblenz and in August 1912 emerged as a Leutnant in the Telegraph Service. So, unlike some of his contemporaries, he did not have the cavalry background which at one time seemed to be a prerequisite for pilot or observer training in the new air service that was beckoning young technically minded soldiers.

Boelcke was well versed in things mechanical, so it is not too surprising that he soon cast his eyes skywards and was accepted for pilot training in June 1914. In August he qualified and joined Flg Abt 13; by early September he was flying an Albatross B 11 with his brother Wilhelm as his observer. In the early days of combat flying, the pilot was considered very much the chauffeur for the gunner/observer, who was looked on as being the more important crew member. The two brothers were so close that the ill-feeling between self-important observers and their so-called 'drivers', which certainly happened in all air services, never occurred. Before long, both men had received decorations for their businesslike work over the Front, Oswald an Iron Cross Second Class in October, and his elder brother a First Class a little later.

The visit of an early Fokker monoplane to his unit in November 1914 fuelled his ambition to become a single-seater fighter pilot, but this was not yet to be. In April 1915 he moved to FLg Abt 62, initially flying LVG B11s but swapping these slow, lumbering aircraft for the new Albatross C 1 when the unit moved to the Front at Douai. The Albatross C 1 was equipped with a Parabellum machine-gun operated by the observer, and on 4 July Boelcke and Lt von Wuehlisch, in the rear cockpit, shot down a French Morane type L parasol, this being Boelcke's first and only victory whilst piloting a two-seater aircraft.

At this time it was usual for all types of reconnaissance, two-seater scouts and single-seaters to be attached to one unit, the prime function of the armed scouts being to protect the unarmed reconnaissance aircraft. Under these circumstances it was not difficult for the 24-year-old Boelcke to sample a Fokker E 1 which had been fitted with the then highly secret synchronization system designed by the Dutch engineer, Anthony Fokker. This mechanism permitted the forward facing guns to fire after the trigger had been pressed only when the propellor had moved out of the line of fire. It was the Dutchman's own design and not in any way based on the system of deflector plates fitted by Roland Garros to his Morane monoplane that had created concern among the ranks of the German fliers during its brief appearance at the Front a few weeks earlier.

Since the gun now fired along the line of flight, it made the pilot's task in aiming and manoeuvring into a firing position much easier, and Boelcke recorded his first solo victory on 19 August.

September saw the embryo ace flying a more powerful Fokker E 11 with which he achieved two victories, and a further pair in October. This new Fokker certainly turned the tables on the French and British, whose pilots became almost paranoiac about what has gone down in the history books as 'the Fokker scourge'. There can be no doubt that the aircraft gave the Germans air superiority, but taken in a total context the reputation was established mainly by Immelmann and Boelcke, as in relative terms there were not very many Fokkers operating in the area at the time; needless to say, those that were did so with great effect.

Boelcke was not a loner, as so many aces proved to be, but was in fact a superb leader of men and a very deep-thinking tactician. In November 1915, he prepared a series of reports for the German supreme headquarters on subjects as diverse as organization, tactics, appraisal of new aircraft and combat summaries. January 1916 brought his eighth victory and with it the award of the Pour le Mérité ('Blue Max'), and his recognition throughout Germany as a national hero.

For a long time he had seen the future of the single-seater fighter as part of a separate fighter unit, and in February 1916 he was given the authority to form small self-contained units of this type for the Verdun Offensive. From these eventually came the *Jagdstaffeln* (fighter squadrons) which started to form in August and of which he commanded *Jasta* 2. Boelcke hand-picked most of the pilots for these new units, and among them was a promising reconnaissance pilot whom he had first met in 1915 when the pilot had been an observer; his name was Manfred von Richthofen.

On 22 May 1916, with his score standing at 18, the Kaiser decreed that Boelcke should receive the rank of Hauptmann; this was the first time a man of 25 of middle class upbringing had achieved such status in the Royal Prussian Army. The following months saw his prestige as a national hero expand further; he was grounded and undertook tours of Germany and other fighting units in the Balkans, Turkey and Russia.

However, the British offensive on the Somme started on 1 July and soon Boelcke was recalled to lead *Jasta* 2. The ascendancy of the Fokker monoplane was passed and Boelcke selected the Fokker D 111 (352/16) as his personal mount. On 17 September 1916 the unit flew the first full-scale sweep over Allied territory, engaging six FE 2s and two BE 2cs of No 11 Squadron RFC. The Germans decimated the British patrol, of which there were no survivors. Also at this time, Boelcke prepared the famous 'Dicta Boelcke' which became the bible of German fighter pilots and was still used by the Luftwaffe in the Second World War.

His score gradually mounted, passing 30 by the end of September and reaching 40 on 25 October when he dispatched a BE 2c over Serre. By now, Boelcke had exchanged his Fokker for an Albatross D1, and the following day he was leading a formation of six aircraft that were stalking a flight of DH 2s. In closing on his leader's aircraft, Lt Boehme—another of Boelcke's protégés—misjudged the gap between the two aircraft and was horrified to see his wing-tip crash into the interplane strut of the black Albatross. Boelcke fought to control the crashing biplane, but it was beyond even his skill and he died as it hit the ground. Boehme was grief stricken at his part in the tragedy, but recovered and went on to achieve 24 victories before dying in combat a year later.

Boelcke was buried with full military honours at Cambrai Cathedral, his decorations being carried before the coffin by von Richthofen.

Although he achieved only half the total that von Richthofen was eventually to record, Boelcke is considered by many to be the best all-round fighter pilot to emerge from the Great War. He displayed tremendous leadership, exceptional flying ability, and possessed a brain that was able to adapt to many levels of tactical and strategic thinking, qualities that many aces possess to some degree but few in the same quantity with which this young Saxon was gifted.

MAX IMMELMANN

(IMPERIAL AIR GERMAN FORCE)

*I*n terms of total victories, Immelmann with 17 is well down the list of First World War aces, but his name is better known than most for the turning manoeuvre with which it is associated. There is no absolute proof that Immelmann ever laid claim to perfecting the turn that has become part of the vocabulary of fighter pilots throughout the world, and it is likely that he was in fact unaware that it was attributed to him.

Born in Dresden on 21 September 1890, he, like Boelcke, was a son of Saxony. His father, a local industrialist, died when Max was seven, and eight years later the young man entered the Saxon Cadet School at Dresden from which he graduated in 1911. Leaving the army a year later, he studied engineering at the Dresden Technical High School, and it was during this period that he visited the flying school at Johannisthal and had his first encounter with the aeroplane. Again, like Boelcke, he was fascinated by all things mechanical, so it is not surprising that when war came in 1914, he applied to join the *Fliegertruppe*.

Mobilized into his old unit, the 2nd Railway Regiment at Schoenberg, he only had to wait until November before his request was granted and he reported to the flying school at Adlershof for pilot training. On passing out in March 1915, he was sent to fly LVG two-seaters, but made an inauspicious start to his career by damaging two in heavy landings. However, in May fate took a hand when he was posted to Flg Abt 62 at Doeberitz where he met Boelcke, and their unique relationship started.

The following month, still flying the LVG reconnaissance aircraft, he encountered combat for the first time when his unarmed aircraft was engaged by a Farman. The Frenchman damaged Immelmann's machine to such an extent that he was forced to make an emergency landing, which he accomplished with great skill. For this feat of airmanship he received the Iron Cross Second Class. He continued to fly two-seater aircraft for a while, but in July the arrival of the Fokker monoplanes saw the start of the much publicized rivalry between him and his friend Boelcke. The two pilots were in fact innocent victims of the media which built up a mythical race towards ace status between them.

On 1 August 1915, Immelmann claimed what is considered to be the very first victory achieved by a single-seater fighter when he intercepted and shot down the BE 2 c of Lt William Reid of No 2 Sqn RFC. So that he could carry a larger bomb load, Reid was flying the BE without an observer, therefore his only defence was manoeuvrability. Immelmann fired sixty rounds before his gun jammed; forty of these hit the British aircraft and wounded the luckless pilot who was forced down. The early chivalry of the air was exhibited by Immelmann when he landed close to Reid and helped him to escape from his damaged aircraft.

Fate played a certain part in the inclusion of this victory in the history books as the first fighter success, for the honour probably belongs to Kurt Wintgens who, on 15 July, claimed a success over French territory but could not confirm his kill with the all-important evidence of the wreckage which was so important to German claims at that time. Nonetheless, Immelmann's name was now on the score sheet and on 25 August he shared another victory with his friend and rival Boelcke when they combined to bring down a Caudron G 1V. Despite this, Immelmann, like many aces, tended to be very much a loner, and he was carrying out a solo patrol the following day when he claimed to have dispatched a single-seater enemy aircraft near Souchez. The RFC, however, reported no losses in that area, so it may have been a French aircraft, although it cannot be ruled out that his adversary escaped by landing and taking off again when the Fokker had departed. This would seem to be the only unconfirmed kill in his total of 17 and probably accounts for why there is still a question mark against his overall score. There was no doubt about his third success on 21 September when a No 10 Sqn RFC BE 2 piloted by Lt Caws fell to the German.

When Boelcke took Flg Abt 62 to Metz, Immelmann was left as the sole defender of the important communications centre at Lille, and his fortitude in carrying out this duty earned him the title of 'The Eagle of Lille'. In October he claimed two further victories which brought him 'ace' status, and in January 1916 he and Boelcke received the Pour Le Mérité which became synonymous with Immelmann when it became universally known as the 'Blue Max'.

It is interesting to note that Immelmann's fourth victim, Captain C. C. Darley of No 11 Sqn RFC, was one of the few RFC officers subsequently to escape from captivity and return to the British lines, going on to command No 88 Sqn in 1918.

Like von Richthofen, Immelmann has been accused of taking easy pickings since most of his victories were against two-seater reconnaissance machines; this is, however, grossly unfair to both men, since it can equally be argued that as they were primarily engaged on defensive patrols it was their job to prevent information from getting back to Allied lines, and their successes certainly achieved this. Immelmann was a master at handling his aircraft, and had tremendous patience in stalking his adversaries. But there were several occasions when he himself was successfully engaged and had to break off combat with damage evident to his aircraft. On two occasions, trouble with his synchronization gear caused him to damage his own propeller and have to force land, and it has been suggested that this may have happened to him on the fateful day he died.

With 15 victories to his credit, and his name a household word in Germany, Immelmann took off in the late afternoon of 18 June 1916 to intercept eight British aircraft which had crossed the line near Arras. He dispatched a No 25 Sqn FE 2b flown by Lt C. S. Rogers to record his 16th success and returned to base. In the evening, he flew again and once more was in combat with No 25 Sqn, this time shooting down the FE 2 of Lt R. B. Savage. However, in so doing he passed in front of Lt G. R. McGubbin's aircraft which turned to follow the German. Immelmann saw the danger, but almost simultaneously Cpl J. Waller, the FE 2's observer, was able to fire a long and accurate burst at the Fokker, which spun to the ground and crashed.

Waller and his pilot did not see any firing from the Fokker's guns during the attack, so the claim that once again Immelmann had shot off his own propeller could not be substantiated, and neither could other German suggestions that the aircraft had suffered structural failure. As was to be the case on many future occasions with other famous airmen, controversy surrounded the death of Germany's first acknowledged ace and national aeronautical hero, who was much respected on both sides of the Front.

MANFRED VON RICHTHOFEN

(IMPERIAL GERMAN AIR FORCE)

Manfred von Richthofen, or to give him his more popular title, the 'Red Baron', has become almost a cult figure, and his exploits, real and imagined, are known to a certain degree to most, however slight their interest in aviation. Yet in some areas there is still not a great deal known about this young nobleman who was by all accounts a man of tremendous courage, with a fascination for killing, very little apparent emotion and a tendency to be very head-strong.

He was the son of a Silesian nobleman and was born on 2 May 1892 in Breslau. He was an average student, but his exceptional marksmanship soon became evident during holidays at the family estate when, together with his brothers, he loved nothing better than to roam the woods hunting.

His Prussian background destined him for a military career, and at the age of 11 he was sent to a military school from which he progressed to the prestigious Royal Prussian Military Academy. Despite popular belief, he was not a fine horseman, making up for what he lacked in ability by his courage and determination. On the outbreak of war, he was serving as a Leutnant with the cavalry and saw action in Poland before moving to the Western Front. By the end of 1915, he was disillusioned with this type of warfare and successfully applied for a transfer to the flying service. After four weeks' training, he qualified as an observer and was soon flying in an Albatross B 11 with one of Germany's first military pilots, Franz Zeumer.

Zeumer was a difficult man to get close to, but he took a liking to the young Uhlan and during periods when they were not on active duty he took Richthofen into the air in a trainer and showed him the basic controls. The man who was destined to become Germany's top ace was, strangely, not a natural pilot and was lucky to survive his first solo in October 1915, when he completely misjudged his approach and made a very heavy landing. However, he persevered and on Christmas Day 1915 qualified as a pilot.

Earlier, during his career as an observer, he had shot down a Farman, but the wreckage fell behind the French lines and could not be confirmed. Similarly, when piloting an early C-type Albatross over the Verdun front on 16 March 1916, he claimed a Nieuport which he hit with a gun he had rigged on his top wing to fire over the propeller arc, but once more the victory was not confirmed. A chance meeting with Boelcke during a train journey when Richthofen was serving as an observer played a great part in his destiny, for when the ace pilot was selecting men to form the nucleus of his new fighter units he once again met the enthusiastic young man of his train journey who was now a pilot, and invited him to join *Jasta* 2.

His first success came during his very first patrol which he undertook with Boelcke and three other newcomers. Flying Albatross D 11s, the Germans encountered a flight of British FE 2s and BE 2cs. Richthofen engaged one of the FEs over Cambrai and mortally wounded its crew; recalling his previous frustration, he landed alongside the downed British machine and cut away the fabric containing its serial. That night he ordered the first of a series of silver cups each of which was to be engraved with the details of his victories, forming a tangible but somewhat macabre record of his prowess.

From this start he never looked back, and his successes have been so well documented that there is little point in going through them in detail once more. It is perhaps worth noting, however, that his eleventh victim on 23 November 1916 was the British ace and Victoria Cross holder, Major Lanoe Hawker, who handled his DH 2 quite brilliantly but in the end succumbed to the superior Albatross D 11. Another peculiar twist of fate was that Lt H. D. Harvey-Kelly, who was the first RFC pilot to land in France after the declaration of war in August 1914, also fell victim to von Richthofen during 1917.

He received the coveted *Pour le Mérité* on 16 January 1917, and at the same time took command of *Jasta* 11. This unit was particularly successful during the Battle of Arras, a period during which Richthofen accounted for 21 aircraft, taking his total beyond Boelcke's 40. On 6 July, he suffered the humiliation of a head wound inflicted by 2nd Lt A. W. Woodbridge of No 20 Sqn flying an FE 2, but this only served to make him a little more cautious, and by 20 April 1918 his total stood at 80. It seemed as though he was invincible and his name was a household word throughout Germany, although he sometimes proved to be very difficult when it came to publicity tours, while on other occasions revelling in them.

On 21 April 1918, the colourful aircraft of *JG* 1, known throughout the Front as 'The Flying Circus', took off with their leader in his red triplane *DR1 425/17* to combat British aerial infiltration in the Villiers-Bretonneux area. Camels of No 209 Sqn engaged the 'Circus', and during the ensuing fight Capt A. R. Brown chased the red triplane to ground level where he claimed to have fired a burst which hit the pilot and forced him to crash. On reaching the downed aircraft, infantrymen found the pilot dead with a bullet wound to the chest.

Claims were subsequently made that this came from ground fire from the 53rd Battalion Australian Field Artillery, but the source of von Richthofen's final fatal injury has never satisfactorily been discovered. The 'Red Baron' was dead and the blow to German morale was tremendous.

Von Richthofen's varying moods, his apparent obsession with decorations and self-glorification coupled with a seeming lack of compassion for his victims, have resulted in the emergence of a fairly unpleasant picture of the man. Consequently, attempts have sometimes been made to belittle his achievements with claims that he simply picked off stragglers and avoided fights whenever he could. As over half of his 80 victims were scouts, and a fair number were well-handled reconnaissance aircraft that put up stern fights before being overcome, this argument does not stand too close a scrutiny. Many other leaders were aloof from their men, but it does not mean to say they did not care or were self-centred. But, as is so often the case with public figures who become legends, they also become 'Aunt Sallys' for sensationalists. That is perhaps another cross that the 'Red Baron' has to bear.

Such is the fascination of the legend of the 'Red Baron' that, 60 years after he was killed in action, the nature of his death still makes the headlines in the national press.

In April 1988 it was widely reported that a letter written by a consultant physician to General Rawlinson's Fourth Army in 1918 had been discovered in a book of poetry. In the letter, written in 1934, Professor John Alexander Nixon recounts how he and a Colonel Sinclair had been called to Bertangles airfield to investigate the various claimants to the victory over the German ace. After describing his findings that von Richthofen had suffered only one fatal bullet wound, the Professor then refers to reports in which the observer of a reconnaissance aircraft claims (sic) 'to have fired a single burst at a German scarlet-painted plane that seemed unaware of the presence of any other plane in the near vicinity . . . so flew alongside and let him have a belt.'

This letter really does not throw any new light whatsoever on who fired the fatal shot. It has long been established that von Richthofen died from a single bullet wound to the chest, so whilst it seems likely that Professor Nixon and Colonel Sinclair, both being doctors, would have been asked to confirm this, it seems odd that either should be asked to arbitrate over the question of who pulled the trigger.

Indeed, it is very likely that at the time no one was particularly bothered. By the mid-1930s, many stories of the Baron's end had originated, and there is fairly strong evidence pointing to Capt Roy Brown, or to a shot fired from the ground. It is well known that in all types of aerial combat there are many claimants to *any* victory. It has also been established that there were many German Scouts painted in bright colours. It seems very likely that when he wrote his letter, Professor Nixon was just relaying one of the many stories that had accumulated over the years. His knowledge of aerial combat and weaponry was probably limited, and it may well be that he felt that since the wound was caused by a .303 calibre bullet, its most likely source was the machine-gun on a reconnaissance aircraft. However, the guns carried by Capt Brown's Camel and the unknown infantryman would also have been of the same calibre. Although every pilot, however experienced, is likely to have lapses in concentration, it seems very unlikely that von Richthofen would have made the basic mistake of which he is accused by the observer. Finally, if he did fire a belt at the range he claims and only one bullet found its mark, it does not say a lot for the arc of fire of his weapon.

Who fired the fatal shot is now never likely to be known, although the odds do seem stacked very much in favour of the lone Australian infantryman in his trench, but such is the power of the legend of the 'Red Baron' that controversy will continue with any new material that is discovered, however long after the events of April 1918 it originates.

ERNST UDET

(IMPERIAL GERMAN AIR FORCE)

With 62 victories credited to him, Udet was second only to von Richthofen with whom he served in the famous 'Flying Circus'. He was the highest-scoring German ace to survive the war, but is remembered more for his activities in the mid-'thirties and his disastrous handling of a variety of administrative posts to which he was appointed by his friend Hermann Goering during the gestation of the 'new' Luftwaffe in the early days of the Second World War.

Udet joined the Imperial German Army in 1914, but in 1915 transferred to the flying service and was trained as a pilot. For a short time he served with Wilhelm Siegert's *Fliegerkorps des Obersten Heeresleitung*, but the 19-year-old was not cut out to be a bomber pilot and soon graduated to the Fokker E 1, scoring his first victory on 18 March 1916 when he shot down a Farman F 40 bomber during a raid on Mulhausen. It was to be seven months before further success came, and this rather slow start continued until May 1917, by which time his score stood at six. In the latter part of 1917 he moved from *Jasta* 15 to *Jasta* 37, and it was then that he started to show his mettle.

Fourteen RFC aircraft fell to his guns between August 1917 and February 1918, and two months later he was honoured by the award of the 'Blue Max'. With his score now at 20, he was moved to *Jasta* 4, which operated mainly on the French Front, and it was with this unit that he took a heavy toll of French aircraft (21) before becoming involved once more against the British, notching 18 RAF aircraft by 26 September (the RAF had been formed on 1 April 1918 by the amalgamation of the RFC and the RNAS). By the time the war ended, he had 62 confirmed kills to his credit and had overtaken his closest rival, Erich Lowenhardt (53), who was killed in August 1918 when his parachute failed to open after a collision with a Fokker D V11.

There was never any doubt about Udet's skill as a superb aerobatic and fighter pilot, testified by the fact that 42 of his victories were against scouts rather than reconnaissance aircraft. But there must remain a huge question mark against his temperament and leadership. Following the death of von Richthofen, he was passed over for command of *JG* 1 which in July went to Hermann Goering and was held by him until the cessation of hostilities in

November.

Udet's love of life and his cavalier approach suited him well in his post-war activities as a stunt and test pilot. Never a political animal, he was, however, in 1935 persuaded by Goering to join the clandestine Luftwaffe. Although he was a deep-thinking extrovert, Udet was just not cut out for office or administration work, and quickly discovered that Goering would not listen or accept facts that he had carefully researched. He was eventually put in charge of aircraft procurement, a fatal move for a man so unsuited to the task.

Easily persuaded to approve changes to existing designs and modifications to armament, he allowed himself to become entangled in a web from which there was no escape. There are many examples of the frustrations he suffered in trying to make Goering understand his depth of perception in analysing situations. On one occasion, he persuaded his chief to experiment with a small force of single-seater fighters to be used in the night fighting role, only to learn that Goering told General Jeschonnek that 'Night fighting will never happen'. He also warned of the growing capacity of the American aircraft industry, which was met with the classic reply, 'It is bluff, my dear Ernst. They can make cars and refrigerators but not aircraft'. Having spent a lot of time in the USA, this last rebuff must have sounded like a death knell to the First World War ace.

It is not surprising, therefore, that three months after this comment, on 17 November 1941, Ernst Udet took his own life. The 44-year-old playboy contributed a great deal to the Fatherland and it would not be an exaggeration to claim that he gave his life for it, although no doubt if given the choice he would have preferred to have died in aerial combat than by his own gun. Apart from being a natural pilot, Udet was also a talented artist and frequently scribbled caricatures of famous people, especially when dining with them. He would no doubt have approved as his epitaph the comment of Fred Schultz, a barman at the Adlon hotel: *'Er ist ein Zerstörer von Tischteuchern'*. Indeed, the delicate hands that had destroyed 62 Allied aircraft had also accounted for a great many tablecloths.

WERNER VOSS

(IMPERIAL GERMAN AIR FORCE)

*V*oss was undoubtedly one of the most skilled pilots to emerge from the First World War, and was at one time von Richthofen's closest rival. Although his career followed similar lines to that of the 'Red Baron' (both originally served in the cavalry and both started their flying careers as observers), he was a much more sensitive man and had great depth of feeling for his opponents. This is reflected in thoughts he penned whilst commanding *Jasta* 10 in July 1917 when he had over 30 victories to his credit. Recalling his days as an observer over the Somme, and feeling melancholy about a BE 2 he had sent crashing to earth, he wrote, 'Poor devils, I know how they felt. I have flown in such a machine. But they spy out our secrets and must be destroyed, but I prefer to shoot down scouts'. At this stage in his career, there is evidence to show that the strain of command was taking its toll although it did not seem to affect his performance as a superlative pilot and excellent marksman, for in the following three months he recorded 14 more victories, ten of which came in a three-week period during September.

Although he is often compared with von Richthofen, his background was entirely different from that of the Prussian aristocrat. His father was an industrialist in Krefeld where Werner was born on 13 April 1897. He had a deep passion for machinery and loved tinkering with his motorcycle; this interest continued throughout his career and it was not unusual to see him wearing a dirty old pair of overalls and getting to grips with the engines of his beloved aeroplanes. Whilst still under age, he enlisted into the Westphalian Hussars, but in August 1915 followed the well-trodden path of many a cavalryman by transferring to the air service.

He flew originally in combat as an observer, which not only cultivated a strong awareness of the importance of such duties, but also a quick eye and a natural bent for aircraft recognition. In the summer of 1916, he applied for pilot training, was accepted, and in November joined *Jasta* 2. On the 27th of that month, just six days after reporting for duty, his name was on the unit's scoreboard when he accounted for a BE 2c. From then on he never looked back, and his skill became known throughout the German air service and the RFC, one of whose most distinguished aces, Major James McCudden, commented that he would never forget the skill of the pilot of the green Fokker Triplane who took on seven SE 5s and managed to hit all of them during a ten-minute running battle. Unknown to McCudden at the time, the airman was Voss.

On 8 April 1917, when his score stood at 28, he was awarded the *Pour le Mérité*, and the following month he took command of *Jasta* 5, before moving on to *Jasta* 29 in July, by which time six more victims had fallen to his guns. Richthofen then invited him to join *JG* 1, and he assumed command of *Jasta* 10.

When the Fokker Dr 1 Triplane arrived on the scene, Voss took an immediate liking to it and was soon in action shooting down five allied aircraft during the first ten days of August. By 23 September, he was due for a much-earned rest and his brothers Otto and Max arrived at Heule to accompany him home to Krefeld. But it was not to be. During the first patrol of the day he shot down a DH 4 which took his score to 48. Then just after six in the evening, he took off once more to try to reach the half century. His enthusiasm to reach this landmark and return home with something really worthwhile to celebrate caused him to abandon his normal caution. Spotting a lone SE 5 heading homewards way below, he failed to consider the likelihood of a trap and angled his Triplane towards the British scout. Above him, however, were six other SE 5s, all from No 56 Sqn and led by the British ace James McCudden. With height and surprise as his two major advantages, the British leader went about his task in a professional and clinical manner.

The SE 5 pilots formed a box blocking the German's escape to the rear, above and below, the only way out being towards the Allied lines. As soon as Voss saw the initial bursts of tracer pass him, he turned the nimble Triplane to face his tormentors, a move that nearly caught them by surprise. The six British pilots were, however, all old hands, and although on three occasions the Fokker pilot did seem to have a clear run for safety, he chose to ignore it and fought valiantly on. A passing formation of Albatrosses tried to intervene, but was held off by a section of SPAD scouts which had arrived on the scene.

The SE 5 pilots wondered just what they had to do to halt this sole German aircraft, but then the fight ended as quickly as it had started. Lt A. P. F. Rhys-David – who eventually scored 23 victories – managed to get the Triplane in his sights. The Old Etonian fired two drums of Lewis gun ammunition into the Fokker, and saw it stagger before diving into the ground and breaking up on impact. This was the RFC pilot's 20th victory, and by the end of the next month he too was dead, but he met his end knowing that his most tenacious victim had been the man that many of his contemporaries considered to be the most skilful and perhaps the most highly respected German pilot of the Great War.

THE SECOND WORLD WAR ACES

GEOFFREY ALLARD

(RAF)

*F*rance, May 1940. The so-called 'Phoney War' had erupted into non-stop action on the 10th and the hard-pressed RAF components of the BEF were fighting a rearguard action against the advancing Germans. At Seclin, No 85 Sqn had fought like tigers and by 17 May their Hurricanes had accounted for 50 enemy aircraft but the action was taking its toll on the pilots. Late in the afternoon of the 17th, a lone Hurricane approached the airfield, landing gear and flaps down, engine throttled back; it wobbled as it made a perfect touch-down and taxied to its dispersal. Groundcrew leaped forward to refuel and rearm the fighter, but the pilot made no attempt to leave it. An airman jumped on to the wing root, looked into the cockpit and found the pilot fast asleep.

The exhausted airman was Sgt Geoffrey Allard, who had scored his first victory on 10 May when he shot down a Heinkel 111 and had become an ace within a week with ten victories to his credit by 17 May. The tremendous efforts made by the RAF pilots in this period reflect the tenacious way in which they fought. The RAF's first ace, Flg Off 'Cobber' Kain, a New Zealander flying with No 73 Sqn, had scored five victories by March 1940 and 17 by 27 May, when he was ordered to England to rest. After taking off, he tried a low-level beat-up of the airfield, but misjudged his roll and was killed when his Hurricane cartwheeled into the ground. No doubt fatigue had some part to play in this fatal error. But Geoffrey Allard, or 'Sammy' as he was known to his friends, was lucky. He was helped from the cockpit of his aircraft and, after a long sleep, was sent home to England the following day.

Allard was a product of Trenchard's Aircraft Apprentice Scheme which had been started in 1920 as part of an overall plan to give the RAF the cream of young men, not only to fly (through Cranwell) but also to maintain and service aircraft to the highest standards. Born in York on 20 August 1912, Allard became a member of the 19th entry at Halton, which he entered on 3 September 1929. Graduating as a metal rigger in August 1932, the young airman made the top grade of Leading Aircraftsman (LAC) during his training, and set about his RAF career from a base that produces the finest airmen in the world. His ultimate ambition was to fly, and by 1936 he had been accepted for pilot training which he undertook at the Bristol Flying

School at Filton. After elementary flying training, he moved to 9 Flying Training School and received his 'wings' on 23 October 1937, at the same time being promoted to Sergeant and being graded 'above average'.

His first posting was to No 85 Sqn, whose famous hexagon marking originated in the 1914-18 war and was carried by its aircraft throughout the Second World War and into the post-war jet age. The Gloster Gladiator with which the squadron was then equipped proved an ideal vehicle for Allard to show his prowess as an aerobatic pilot, and he soon established himself as a leader in this field and was regarded by all as a 'natural'. His progression through Halton, four years as a serving airman and then into the jealously guarded ranks of aircrew, stood him well. He was much liked by all ranks on the squadron and had the strength of character that was to be found in the majority of the so-called 'Trenchard Brats'.

Equipped with Hurricanes and under the command of Sqn Ldr David Atcherley (later AVM and AOC No 205 Group, killed in a Meteor PR 10 on 7 June 1952), No 85 Sqn moved to France on 9 September 1939, at which time Allard was flying with 'A' Flight. The squadron flew patrols of varying natures until 10 May when the blitzkrieg against the Low Countries commenced. On returning from France, No 85 had established a record of which it could be proud: in 11 days' fighting they had accounted for 89 enemy aircraft. On the debit side, they had lost two pilots killed, six wounded and nine missing. Allard's ten victories earned him a DFM which was gazetted on 31 May, the day before he was promoted to Flight Sergeant and returned to the squadron which was now under the command of Sqn Ldr Peter Townsend.

The summer months saw No 85 deeply involved in what has become known as the Battle of Britain and, not unexpectedly, 'Sammy' Allard was to the fore, recording his eleventh victory, a He 111, on 8 July and claiming another of the same type as a probable on the following day. Patrolling with Flt Lt Hamilton on the 30th of that month, he shared two Bf 110s and, nine days later with Sgts Ellis and Evans, he accounted for a Dornier Do 17 near Lowestoft.

On 17 August 1940, Allard was commissioned and two days later the squadron moved to Croydon. Almost as if to celebrate this double event, the now Pilot Officer Allard started a run which brought him ten victories in nine days. Although downing a Bf 109 on 24 August, the main task of the Hurricanes was to go for the Luftwaffe's bombers.

In this, Allard and his fellow pilots excelled; on 30 August, 11 Hurricanes attacked a force of 50 He 111s escorted by Bf 109s flying at some 16,000 feet over Bethersden. Although outnumbered by at least ten to one, the British fighters tore into the bombers and Allard soon had a He 111 in his sights; a burst from his eight Brownings sent the bomber staggering before rolling on to its back and plummeting earthwards with both engines flaming. A similar fate awaited the second, which came to earth near the Squadron's base at Croydon. Other actions followed throughout August, and Allard was rarely off the score sheet, his prowess as a pilot being supported by his unerring marksmanship. On 1 September he scored his

25th and last victory when he chased a Bf 109 across the Channel and, with the French Coast in sight, hit it with one burst of fire from about 100 yards, sending it to a watery end.

No 85 moved via Castle Camps to Church Fenton where it was told that it was to become a night fighter squadron. Allard was promoted to Flight Lieutenant and took command of 'A' Flight. By now he also had a Bar to his DFM, as well as a DFC.

The squadron moved to Kirton-in-Lindsey on 23 October and began to receive American-manufactured Douglas Havoc night fighters. It was only to be expected that 'Sammy' Allard directed all his energy into mastering the heavy twin and encouraging the pilots of 'A' Flight to do the same. Operating from Debden, Allard could not get his hands on the Havocs fast enough, and as soon as he knew aircraft were ready at the MUs he arranged ferry flights.

It was such a flight that brought about his death. On 13 March 1941, he learned that two new aircraft were ready for collection at Ford. Arriving at the dispersal at Debden with Plt Off W. Hodgson and Sgt F. Walker-Smith, he found an airman struggling to fasten a nose panel on Havoc *BJ500*. He immediately took the screwdriver and fixed the panel, no doubt relishing this momentary return to his days as a rigger. It proved a fatal move. As the Havoc's nose-wheel left the Debden runway, the panel came adrift, flew back over the cockpit and jammed the rudder. The heavy fighter flicked into a roll and ploughed upside-down into the ground where it exploded in a ball of flame, instantly killing the three occupants.

There can be little doubt that if Allard had not met his end in this way he would have continued to add to his score as a night fighter pilot, and could possibly have become another of the graduates from the Aircraft Apprentice School at Halton to achieve very senior rank.

GEORGE BEURLING

(RAF)

*P*robing the bottom of a 26-feet deep hole, the mechanical digger at last struck something very solid. Members of the Fenland Aircraft Preservation Society were about to have their tenacity and effort rewarded with the recovery of a Spitfire Mk 11 Merlin engine, as well as other valuable relics that had been buried in the marshy field at Middle Drove, near Wisbech, Cambridgeshire, for 42 years. So why, in 1985, did the excavation of this particular Spitfire have any more interest than others that had been recovered by various groups since aviation archaeology became part of the preservation scene? The answer is that the pilot of Spitfire *P7913 'City of Birmingham'*, on the occasion of its last flight on 8 June 1943, was the Canadian-born ace Sqn Ldr George Frederick Beurling, arguably the RAF's most successful exponent of deflection shooting.

The Spitfire Beurling was flying was a tired machine. It was built in December 1940, had served with Nos 66 and 118 Sqns, and was now being used at Sutton Bridge, a gunnery school. Believing the aircraft to be so worn out that it represented a danger to any inexperienced pilot who might be detailed to fly it, Beurling had used it for a tactical exercise and, after about one hour's flying, had baled out and left it to dig a very deep hole for itself in the Cambridgeshire fens. His story was that the engine had caught fire due to a coolant leak, but privately he let slip that he had in fact deliberately crashed the aircraft. This could well have been another of the apocryphal stories that surrounded the Canadian loner, but when the FAPS members cleaned and examined the Merlin, they found much evidence of wear, but no trace of fire. So, 37 years after his death in a flying accident in 1948, another piece of evidence was produced to explain why Beurling was affectionately known as 'Screwball'.

Born in Verdun, Manitoba, in 1922, Beurling was besotted with flying from a very early age, and by the time he was 15 had accumulated over 150 hours, passed all his examinations for a commercial licence but was still too young to hold one. After an ill-fated attempt to become a mercenary in China, he volunteered to join the RCAF when war broke out in September 1939, but found his academic qualifications too low for pilot training, a bitter lesson resulting from having left school at 15 to earn money to pay for flying instruction. However, he signed on as a deck-hand aboard a Glasgow-

Above *The beautifully cowled rotary engine of the Fokker E 1 with Ltn Max Immelmann in the cockpit* (Author's collection).

Right *Ltn Max Immelmann whose name is perpetuated in the manoeuvre known as the 'Immelmann turn'* (Chaz Bowyer).

Left *Oberleutnant Ernst Udet with his Pour le Merité ('Blue Max') at his throat* (Chaz Bowyer).

Below *The Channel Front, 4 September 1940. General Oberst Ernst Udet (centre) with Luftwaffe aces (l–r) Wilhelm Balthasar, KIA 3/7/41, Walter Oesau, KIA May 1944, Adolf Galland, Ernst Udet, Werner Mölders, unknown, Hartmann Grasser* (Chaz Bowyer).

Right *A Fokker E 111 monoplane creates a miniature dust storm during take-off* (Dr Volker Koos).

Below right *An Albatros-built Fokker D V11* (Author's collection).

Left *Ltn Werner Voss who was awarded his Pour le Merité in April 1917* (via Chaz Bowyer).

Below left *Major James T. B. McCudden VC DSO★ MC★ MM, killed when he made a very basic flying error on 9 July 1918 when returning to France to assume command of No 60 Sqn* (via Chaz Bowyer).

Below *Flt Lt Geoffrey 'Sammy' Allard DFC DFM of No 85 Sqn* (via Chaz Bowyer).

Above *Flg Off George Beurling with Capt Roy Brown DSC, the man credited with shooting down von Richthofen in April 1916.*

Right *Wing Commander J. R. D. 'Bob' Braham DSO DFC, a Mosquito pilot credited with 19 night and 10 day victories* (via Norman Franks).

Above *Wing Commander Frank Carey DFC★★ AFC DFM* (via Chaz Bowyer).

Left *Pierre Clostermann DFC. The Second World War French ace takes time off to feed some foraging geese* (via Norman Franks).

Above right *Pierre Clostermann in the cockpit of his Tempest* Le Grand Charles (via Chaz Bowyer).

Right *Gus Daymond (left) and Chesley Petersen of No 71 Eagle Sqn, 1941* (via Norman Franks).

bound cargo ship and, on arrival, immediately volunteered to join the RAF.

Told that he must have his parents' consent and his birth certificate, neither of which he possessed, he re-joined the cargo boat, returned to Canada, and repeated the process. One week later he was back in the recruiting office. Following his rejection by the RCAF, the young Beurling had left nothing to chance and had spent time on extra studies that had brought him up to the required educational standard. Such tenacity was to be highlighted on many more occasions during the next five years.

His RAF pilot training started on 7 September 1940, and one year later Sgt Pilot Beurling joined No 403 Sqn. Ironically, this unit was soon to become a Canadian Squadron and, as he was a member of the RAF, Beurling was posted to No 41 Sqn, where he was credited with two FW 190s in May. However, his tendency to break formation and chase enemy aircraft by himself was not well received, and in June he applied, and was accepted, for transfer to No 249 Sqn based in Malta.

Beurling was one of the RAF pilots who flew Spitfires from the deck of HMS *Eagle* to the beleaguered island, and it was there that he found his true niche. On the very afternoon of his arrival, the squadron was in action and Beurling was to the forefront. His first encounter was with a Bf 109, at which he fired but could not confirm as another latched on to his tail; in avoiding this, he found himself well placed behind a Macchi 202 which shuddered as the Spitfire's 20 mm shells hit it, but again he did not see it crash as he set off in pursuit of a section of Ju 88s attacking Valetta. He then received a desperate call for help from a fellow pilot who was trying to land but had a Bf 109 on his tail, so Beurling immediately set off and shot down the enemy fighter – his first confirmed kill in Malta. Short of fuel and ammunition, Beurling was forced to land, but within an hour was airborne again, this time intercepting Ju 87s that were attacking shipping. Within moments, the sky was full of Bf 109s trying to protect the dive-bombers. Beurling immediately downed a fighter then damaged a Ju 87, pieces of which hit his Spitfire, forcing him into an emergency landing.

His first day on the island had been a true baptism of fire during which he had added three enemy aircraft to his score and had probably accounted for two more. Almost as if to recognize the arrival of the Spitfires, there was a lull in the air fighting for most of June, during which time Beurling practised deflection shooting at sand lizards with his pistol. The following month the assault started again, and on the 11th he downed three Macchi 202s and earned himself a DFM. Success followed at a prodigious rate, his phenomenal eyesight, superb marksmanship and hunting instinct more than compensating for his only average ability as a pilot.

By October 1942, the Mediterranean skies were secure in the hands of the Allies, and on the 15th Beurling flew his last sortie from Malta. He intercepted and shot down a Ju 88, taking his total over the island to 26, and overall to 28, but in the combat he was slightly injured in his right foot.

Two weeks later he was aboard a Liberator *en route* to England when the aircraft crashed during the approach to Gibraltar. Beurling was near an escape hatch and managed to extricate himself from the sinking bomber and swim ashore; one of only 24 survivors. He eventually reached Canada where he was greeted as a national hero, but all the time he was anxious to return to the fighting, which he did with No 412 Sqn at the end of 1943.

As a Flight Commander, he was very much involved in leading large sections of Spitfires in sweeps over France but found this very tiresome and limiting. He was also the squadron's gunnery officer, but found it difficult to impart his knowledge of marksmanship to the younger pilots, probably because it was a natural instinct that could not be taught. By the end of the war he had added three more FW 190s to his tally, making his final score 31, together with a share in a Ju 88.

He was now a Squadron Leader with a DSO, DFC, DFM and Bar to his credit, but could not adjust to civilian life. He tried several jobs including selling insurance, touring as a stunt pilot, and commercial flying, but he still yearned for adventure. In 1948 he volunteered to serve as a mercenary with the new state of Israel which had already recruited several of his Canadian colleagues to fly Spitfires. On 20 May 1948, he was asked to fly a Norseman from Rome to Israel, and was given instruction on this type by a former Canadian Navy pilot. With both men on board, the aircraft took off to practice circuits and landings. Witnesses saw it stall on its first overshoot and plunge to the ground, killing both occupants. At the age of 26, 'Screwball' Beurling's luck had finally run out.

JOHN BRAHAM

(RAF)

*I*t is common in most services for people to end up with some form of nickname, often based on some distinctive activity, an abbreviation of the surname, a characteristic or for some other often intangible reason. Most are fairly obvious, but in the case of John Braham, the sobriquet 'Bob' by which he was better known, had no more sinister origin than the fact that there were so many Johns on his first squadron (No 29) at a time when it was customary to use first names as callsigns that he chose to use the diminutive version of his second name, Robert.

Like many other youngsters of their era, Braham's enthusiasm for flying had been fed by a diet of the exploits of Ball, McCudden, Mannock et al, so it is not difficult to appreciate the disappointment felt by the embryo fighter pilot when, on getting his 'wings' on 28 August 1938, his first posting was to a two-seater night fighter squadron. The young pilot officer made several requests for transfer to a single-seater day fighter squadron, but these were not granted, so he settled down to flying the cumbersome turret-armed Demon biplanes, later converting to the stop-gap Blenheim Mk 1F night fighter.

Both aircraft in the 20-year-old's eyes were far removed from the Furys he had so enjoyed flying at No 11 FTS. As he trundled the Blenheim around the sky, envying the Hurricane pilots of Nos 85 and 87 Sqns who shared Debden with No 29 Sqn, there were many occasions when he thought of his initial ambition to join the Colonial Police. This had been followed by a decision to escape the boredom of a temporary office job by joining the Merchant Navy, a move frowned on by his father, a vicar which prompted a rather 'spur of the moment' decision to volunteer for the expanding RAF's new short service commission scheme in 1938. Although rather slow to master the intricacies of *ab initio* on Tiger Moths – taking 14 hours dual before the magic first solo – he proved to be a good pilot with a natural feel for gunnery. Nonetheless, it would have been difficult to forecast that he was destined to become the RAF's most decorated fighter pilot and the Service's top-scoring night fighter ace.

The first of his 29 victims fell to the guns of his Blenheim on 24 August 1940 when he intercepted a Do 17 coned by searchlights over the Humber. On this occasion he was flying a non-radar-equipped aircraft, and although he damaged the 'bogey' with his forward firing under-belly gun-pack, it was Sgt Wilsden in the Blenheim's turret who completed the destruction. On 2 September, No 29 took delivery of their first Beaufighter and this powerful twin with its cannon armament was more akin to the nimble fighters after which Braham still hankered. It took a little while for the crews to get acclimatized to the 'box of tricks' known as AI (Airborne Interception) radar that enabled the Beau to see in the dark, for although this had been installed in very basic form in both Defiants and Blenheims, the higher performance envelope of the Beaufighter made it an entirely different proposition.

There were of course teething troubles both with the cannons and the AI, and Braham and his radar operator Sgt Ross suffered many frustrations before the now Flg Off Braham scored his second kill. This came on the night of 13 March 1941 when a perfect radar interception placed the Beau 400 yards behind a Dornier 17. Braham fired at the bomber only to have his cannons jam after the opening burst. Ross struggled to clear the fault as Braham kept the bomber in sight, and such was the determination of the pilot that he eventually decided to ram the Dornier. When warned of this rather drastic measure, Ross suggested one more attempt with the cannons which this time obliged and blew the Dornier and its luckless crew to pieces.

Soon after this, Braham recorded a victory of another kind when he married a young nurse, the ceremony being conducted by his father and marked by a fly-past by No 29 Sqn, an honour that not many pilots could claim in war-torn Britain. The Braham/Ross partnership, now operating from West Malling, claimed three more victims, including a pair of Heinkels in one sortie, before Sgt Ross was rested.

His place was taken by Sgt 'Sticks' Gregory, and the new partnership put their names on the scoreboard on 6 July when a Ju 88, after a brave fight by its crew, fell to their guns over the Thames estuary. Braham's score mounted throughout 1941, during which time he spent a short time with No 141 Sqn and then moved on to No 51 OTU. It was whilst with the latter during June 1942 that he made a 'social' visit to No 29 Sqn during which he persuaded the CO to let him take a Beau with the new AI Mk 7 radar on a sortie. This proved successful when he accounted for a Do 17, but deteriorating weather forced him to divert to Manston where he clipped a building on landing and severely damaged the borrowed aircraft.

Ironically, at the end of the month, now a Squadron Leader with two DFCs, he and Gregory (now commissioned) were posted back to No 29 where they selected Beaufighter *V8284* as their aircraft. On 9 August they demonstrated that they had not lost their finely honed edge when they shot down a Do 17, followed by two more confirmed and three damaged before the end of the month. One of these combats serves to indicate the narrow margin which often separated a pilot from an untimely end and a long fighting career. One of the Ju 88s intercepted by Braham succeeded in setting his aircraft on fire, forcing him to force land on a small emergency strip near Beachy Head. Inspection of the Beaufighter the following morning showed that a cannon shell from the German aircraft had missed the back of Braham's seat by inches.

In October he was awarded the DSO, then in December his career took a dramatic turn with promotion to Wing Commander and the command of No 141 Sqn at Ford. On moving to Predannack in Cornwall for operations over the Bay of Biscay, Braham continued to score regularly, and in addition to enemy bombers occasionally went hunting U-boats and E-boats, causing several of the former to seek the sanctuary of the depths, and sending one of the latter, much to the chagrin of its crew, the same way! The sinking of the E-boat brought him his third DFC. By now, No 141 was fully refreshed for full-scale operations, and Braham was given permission to start night and day intruder missions over France attacking aircraft, U-boats, railway and transport installations and targets of opportunity.

In the summer of 1943, 'Serrate' radar, which enabled the crew to home in on the emissions of German night fighters' radar, was fitted to the Beaufighters and a system whereby the aircraft operated with the bomber streams was introduced. During the Peenemunde raid on 17 August, Braham proved the worth of the radar when he shot down the Bf 110s of Feldwebel Heinz Vinke (54 victories) and Oberfeldwebel Georg Kraft (15 victories); a third German ace, Hauptmann August Geiger (53 victories) fell to Braham on 29 September. He now had twenty kills to his credit.

A Staff College course interrupted his flying, and an appointment to No 2 Group's Operational Staff could have led to a comparatively quiet end to his war. However, he flew whenever he could and on 12 May 1944 nearly met his end when his Mosquito was damaged by a Bf 109 and he was forced to ditch some 70 miles from home. Safely picked up by the Air Sea Rescue Service, he received a dressing down from his AOC, Air Vice Marshal Basil Emburey, for exceeding his operational 'ration' and was grounded until D-Day.

Later that month he was awarded a second Bar to his DSO, and to celebrate this took a No 21 Sqn Mosquito on an intruder mission. The aircraft was detected by radar and a pair of FW 190s led by Leutnant Robert Spreckles of *JG* 1 ambushed the British aircraft. Braham fought hard but became Spreckles' 45th victim, spending the rest of the war with his navigator, Don Walsh, in Stalag Luft 3 at Sagan.

Released in May 1945, Wing Commander Braham was awarded a permanent commission but found it hard to settle to routine peacetime duties and in 1946 resigned only to re-enlist when he found civilian life also not to his taste. Six years later he moved his family to Canada and transferred to the RCAF where he eventually commanded a jet fighter squadron.

FRANK CAREY

(RAF)

Sqn Ldr Frank Carey, the commanding officer of No 135 Sqn, was depressed. He had recently arrived in Burma with his squadron but had no aircraft, and he and his pilots were anxious to join in the air fighting. Consequently, on 28 January 1942, he set out from his temporary headquarters at Ziatquin to visit his old friend Sqn Ldr 'Bunny' Stone whose No 17 Sqn Hurricanes were operating from Mingaladon. He told 'Bunny' that he was browned off with hearing about other people shooting down Japanese aeroplanes and asked if he could fly with No 17 on their next sortie. Always happy to help a friend, Stone agreed, and at about 1100 hours the squadron was brought to readiness. Carey took off with Stone and was soon in the thick of a swirling mass of Japanese fighters and bombers. He managed to get a Nakajima Ki 27 in his sights and after a hectic chase during which he saw his bullets tear into the flimsy Japanese aircraft, he watched it crash into a parked Blenheim at Mingaladon.

It was his first victory in the Far East, and within a month he was to be promoted to Wing Commander in charge of the Mingaladon Wing. Several reports claim that the Japanese pilot of the Ki 27 had 27 bullet wounds, and that the incident had occurred on 29 January, but copies of Sqn Ldr Stone's personal diary which are in the possession of the author, make no mention of the number of hits, simply stating that '. . . on 28th Frank did some of my readiness and shot down his first type 27, the pilot of which had several bullet wounds'.

Whether it was 28 or 29 January, and how many wounds the pilot suffered, are to a degree unimportant. Of more significance is a later entry in the diary which clearly underlines Stone's respect for Carey and his opinion that he was one of the best pilots and marksmen produced by the RAF, with a final total much higher than that with which he was credited, comments that endorse the feelings of many who have looked at the career of Frank 'Chota' Carey.

Born in London on 7 May 1912, Carey followed a route very similar to that of Geoffrey Allard. He became a 'Trenchard Brat' and graduated from the 16th Entry at Halton as a metal fitter, joining No 43 Sqn at Tangmere to service their Siskin fighters. His ambition to fly was realized in 1935, and he graduated from No 6 Flying Training School Netheravon as a Sergeant

Pilot with an 'above average' rating in 1936. To his undisguised delight, he was posted to 'A' Flight of No 43 Squadron flying Hawker Fury fighters. His prowess as an aerobatic pilot was soon apparent, and in the halcyon days of the late 'thirties he represented the squadron at many of the then popular air pageants.

Gathering war clouds saw No 43 become one of the first units to be equipped with the monoplane Hurricane fighter in late 1938, and by the time war was declared nine months later the squadron was very familiar with the eight-gunned fighter. Early patrols brought little action and it was not until 29 January 1940 that Carey first tasted combat when, with Flt Lt Caesar Hull and Plt Off North, he attacked a Heinkel 111 near Hartlepool; the German bomber escaped into cloud and the three Hurricanes returned to Acklington from which No 43 had been operating since the previous November.

The next day, again flying as number 2 to Hull, a pair of He 111s that were attacking a small fishing trawler were intercepted and the Hurricanes shot one of them into the sea, then watched as the German bomber's erstwhile victim rescued the crew of five, an early lesson in the vagaries of war for the RAF pilots. Carey had to be content with further shared victories which brought him a DFM in March, then on 1 April he was commissioned and posted to No 3 Squadron flying Hurricanes out of Kenley.

On 10 May, the war in France finally became serious and No 3 was dispatched to Merville to reinforce the RAF's fighter squadrons trying to stem the German advance. It was on this day that Carey scored his first 'solo' victory when he single-handedly tackled a Heinkel 111 that was part of a mass formation. Four Ju 87s and a Do 17 on 12 and 13 May brought him 'ace' status, but on the 14th he was injured when the gunner of a Dornier 17 he attacked continued firing at his Hurricane until he died as the Dornier ploughed into the ground. Carey was forced to land his damaged fighter near Brussels, where his leg wound was treated by soldiers manning a first-aid post. He then hitch-hiked into Brussels to get fuller medical attention. He eventually managed to get a lift back to England and on reporting to his unit discovered that he had been posted as 'missing believed killed in action'.

He was, however, a long way from being finished, and in June, now a Flight Lieutenant with two DFCs to his credit, he once again joined No 32 as 'A' Flight commander. His arrival was timely, for the Battle of Britain was about to begin. Carey fought throughout the campaign, being wounded twice; by 18 August, when he flew his last sortie in the Battle, his tally had risen to 18.

He experienced many unusual adventures, one of which occurred when he joined up with what he thought were Hurricanes only to discover they were Bf 109s. The German pilots did not immediately spot the lone Hurricane, but a patrolling Bf 110 did and engaged Carey from behind, hitting his port wing ammunition tank and causing the Hurricane to flip on to its back. Carey wisely decided to head for home, but in so doing was then shot at by the Tangmere defences. Eventually he landed successfully, and the Hurricane was repaired. On 18 August, after downing a Ju 87, he suffered bullet wounds to his right knee and crash-landed at Pulborough, subsequently being treated at the Royal Sussex Hospital. In November, he joined No 52 OTU as an instructor, but soon moved to No 245 charged with the defence of Belfast. Again this was a short stay, and he was promoted to Squadron Leader to take over No 135 Sqn which was detailed to move to the Far East in December.

During his period in Burma, Carey added at least ten Japanese aircraft to his score, and earned for himself a reputation for marksmanship and leadership that was to see him appointed OC Air Fighting Training Unit at Amarda. His small stature resulted in the nickname 'Chota' ('Little One'), but there was nothing small about his contribution to the training of embryo operational pilots. Promotion to Group Captain came in 1944, soon after which he moved to the Middle East. In 1945, already holding three DFCs and a DFM, he was awarded an AFC, and in July he returned to England to serve with the Central Fighter Establishment.

Awarded a permanent commission, he served both on flying and administrative duties until June 1960 when he left the RAF and moved to Australia, a country with which he had fallen in love during a spell as Air Adviser to the High Commissioner in 1958. The day after his retirement he was awarded a very much deserved CBE. In most historians' minds, there is little doubt that his final tally was much higher than his official 28; there is also little doubt that he was one of the RAF's greatest fighter pilots.

PIERRE CLOSTERMAN

(RAF)

*I*t cannot be overstated that it is almost impossible to find any single factor that is a vital ingredient to the success of any ace, apart, that is, from luck, and that plays a part in every aspect of life. Lady Luck looked providentially on many aces, and without her intervention it is clear that a number of them would never have achieved 'ace' ranking or even survived. On the other side of the coin, there were those who survived everything the enemy could throw at them only to perish as the result of a moment's lapse or ill-fortune when luck was looking the other way.

One man on whom this fate could easily have fallen in a most ironical way was Frenchman Pierre Closterman, who excelled not only in aerial combat but also in ground strafing. Four days after peace was declared in Europe, he was taking part in a victory fly-past over Bremerhaven when he collided with another participant and had to make his first parachute descent; and, if that was not enough, just over a month later he was involved in a crash landing. So, in a very short space of time after the cessation of hostilities, he came as close to death as he had throughout his combat career which started in the summer of 1943 at RAF Biggin Hill.

Closterman was a Frenchman living in Brazil at the start of the war. He reached England in 1942 and immediately volunteered for service with the RAF, joining No 341 'Alsace' Squadron of the Free French Air Force as a sergeant pilot in 1943. Flying Spitfire IXs under the command of Réné Mouchotte, who had moulded the unit into an efficient fighting force, No 341 was involved in low-level sweeps over the Channel as well as escort duties, and this variety of action gave Closterman the experience he turned to such tremendous advantage later in the war when he was primarily engaged with tactical support flying Typhoons and Tempests.

He already had several operational trips to his credit when, on 27 July 1943, he opened his account with a pair of the formidable FW 190s that had proved more than a match for the British Spitfire when they had first entered service, and had been one reason why the improved Spitfire IX that Closterman was flying had been developed so urgently. One month later he shot down another FW 190 and followed this on 26 September with a Bf 109 to celebrate the award of his commission.

Posted to No 602 Sqn, Closterman was very much involved with the squadron's working-up period in which embryo members of the 2nd Tactical Air Force undertaking low-level flying with Spitfire Vs played an important part. In early 1944, he returned to flying the later mark of Spitfire, and was involved in attacking V1 rocket sites. This tended to curtail his air-to-air combat opportunities, but whenever they arose he took full advantage and by July had shot down three more Bf 109s and a couple of FW 190s, and had been awarded a DFC. On 2 July, he became one of the first Allied pilots to encounter the new long-nosed FW 190D ('Dora') fighters, and although his Spitfire was outclassed by this latest weapon in the Luftwaffe's inventory, his skill overcame that of the German pilots and two victories took his total to ten.

Just as he was getting a fresh taste for aerial combat, he was brought back from France to serve in the HQ of the Free French Air Force, as well as attending a course at the Advanced Gunnery School at Catfoss where he joined such elite company as 'Screwball' Beurling, 'Sailor' Malan and, for a short time, the American ace, Richard Bong. By the end of 1944, he managed to get back to an operational unit and joined 122 Tempest Wing at Volkel in 1945. He became a flight commander with No 274 Sqn and had a traumatic debut with the big Hawker fighter when on his first sortie he was badly shot up and saw his squadron commander, Sqn Ldr D. Fairbanks, killed.

The Tempest, however, was much to his liking, and soon the extrovert Frenchman was extracting every ounce of performance from it, being equally at home engaged in combat or in strafing enemy airfields and troop columns. He added steadily to his score and, although he was slightly wounded after a move to No 56 Sqn in March, and survived a crash-landing on 2 April, his spirit was undaunted. His final operational posting was to No 3 Squadron, where in the last few days of the war he took his final tally to 19 confirmed kills with three FW 190s, two Do 24s and a Ju 52; he is also credited with five probables and eight damaged. His other victories included Ju 88s, He 111s, a Fi 156, a Ju 290, a Ju 252 and, on the ground, several Ar 232s, He 177s and Ju 188s, and on water, Do 24s, Do 18s and BV 138s. In his 293 operational sorties, he also destroyed, in addition to aircraft, 72 trains, 225 vehicles and two boats.

So, variety was very much the spice of life as far as this particular French ace was concerned. After the war, Closterman left the RAF as a Squadron Leader, and turned to politics, becoming a member of the French House of Representatives; he also served with the Armée de l'Air throughout the crises in Algeria.

GREGORY 'GUS' DAYMOND

(RAF)

*T*he new vogue for flying took America by storm, just as it had spread through Europe, and after the First World War there were many colourful characters who made a good but sometimes dangerous living in what has become known as 'barnstorming', as well as opening up the American continent to air travel with early mail flights over staged routes, and later passenger flying. Consequently, when the war in Europe began in 1939, there were many American pilots who recalled the days of the *Lafayette Escadrille* of the First War, and could not get to England fast enough to offer their services to the RAF.

One such pilot was 20-year-old Gregory Daymond, who had learned to fly at his own expense and acquired considerable experience in South America and South Africa, but, at the time that war was declared, was a make-up artist with Warner Brothers in Hollywood. This colourful character, known to everyone as 'Gus', made his way to England and in 1941 was one of the American volunteers who formed No 71 (Eagle) Squadron, one of three RAF squadrons using this name and manned by American pilots. In September 1942, the squadrons were transferred to the USAAC, but not before they and the pilots had carved their own unique niche in the history of the RAF.

Before the formation of the 'Eagle' squadrons, seven American volunteers had served with Fighter Command during the Battle of Britain, six of them losing their lives in the defence of Britain. Serving with Nos 64, 151, 601, 609 and 616 Sqns, the first to be killed in action on 17 August 1940 was Plt Off 'Billy' Fiske. The first 'Eagle' ace of the war was William Dunn, who was wounded soon after claiming his fifth victory in August 1941, and added no further kills to his total.

Pilot Officer Daymond completed his training on Hurricanes and started operational flying with No 71 Sqn in April 1941, being mainly engaged on escort duties during sweeps into France. He had to wait until 2 July before his first kill, when a Bf 109E fell foul of 12 'Eagle' Sqn Hurricanes airborne from North Weald. Plt Off Hall was shot down, but Daymond was quick to avenge his colleague, and four days later showed he had acquired a taste for this type of action when he accounted for another Bf 109 over Northern France. A month later, almost to the day, he found a

Dornier Do 17 skimming low over the Channel, and although the German rear gunner put up a spirited defence, his guns soon fell silent as the American closed in. A well-directed burst from his guns sent the bomber bouncing off the water, and as it rose again the American hit it once more and watched as it plunged below the surface, leaving just a trail of bubbles, oil and debris.

This was the only bomber to fall to Daymond, his fourth victory being yet another Bf 109, this time an 'F' version which he shot down near Mazingarbe on 4 September. During that month, No 71 re-equipped with Spitfire Vs and it was whilst flying *AB812* on a 'Rhubarb' on 19 September that the American had his closest call. Accompanied by Flg Off Johnnie Flyn, he set out to find suitable targets to harass but found little of interest until, on the way home, the pair spotted an airfield from which a couple of Bf 109s were taking off. The Spitfires attacked the German fighters without success, but as they evacuated the target area, six more Bf 109s fell on them. The Germans were no better marksmen than the two 'Eagles', but their unexpected arrival surprised the Spitfire pilots to such an extent that they became separated.

Flynn received the attention of two Bf 109s whilst the remaining four made off after Daymond. The four German fighters took it in turns to get on to the Spitfire's tail as the American tried every trick in the book to shake them off. But his task looked hopeless as by now he was right down on the sea and the Bf 109s had boxed him in. The Spitfire's propeller was throwing spray over the aircraft and bullets from the Germans began to find their mark, one burst tearing off the British fighter's hood. In desperation, 'Gus' closed his throttle and skidded his aircraft sideways, a manoeuvre which took the Bf 109s completely by surprise.

They all shot past, and as they did so the American reacted like lightning, banging the throttle fully open and correcting the skid with deft use of his rudder and ailerons. He now found a 109 ahead of him and a burst from his cannons sent the German fighter cartwheeling into the Channel – victory no 5, and he was an ace. He managed to record hits on a second 109, but with fuel now limited the German pilots broke off the engagement and turned for home. This action resulted in the award of a DFC on 4 October.

Another 'Eagle', Flt Lt Chesley Petersen, became CO of No 71 in November, and it was whilst he was leading the squadron on 8 December that Daymond accounted for another Bf 109 during a strafing run. It was also at this time that he was rested from ops and went on a tour of fighter units in America with Wing Commander Al Deere, returning to No 71 as a flight commander in April 1942.

On 1 June he was once again fighting for his life, this time over Ostend, when his formation was bounced by at least 50 FW 190s. His wing man, Plt Off George Teicheira, was shot down and 'Gus' was left with five hungry FW 190s to fend off. He hit several before managing to get away from their unwanted attention, and landed at Manston completely exhausted and with barely enough fuel to wet the bottom of his tanks. He claimed a probable, but two other pilots had seen a FW 190 plunge into the sea at about the time of the combat, so he was credited with a further victory.

He flew four patrols during the ill-fated Dieppe operation, and soon afterwards took over command of No 71 from Petersen. In September 1942, the three RAF 'Eagle' squadrons were absorbed into the 8th Air Force, but before swopping the RAF blue and the rank of Squadron Leader for the USAAC khaki and the title Major, he received a Bar to his DFC. His kills stood at seven air and one ground, together with a damaged, and he did not add to these whilst serving in the USAAC. Daymond survived the war and retired from the American Air Force as a Lieutenant Colonel to become an executive in the American electronics industry.

TONY EYRE

(RAF)

*I*t became obvious in the mid-1930s that Britain must increase the strength of its defences, and that included the RAF which had been allowed to become a mere shadow, if not in quality then certainly in quantity, of the powerful air force that existed at the end of the Great War. The initial emphasis was on new aircraft, followed closely by the training of men to fly them. At that time the biplane still reigned supreme, and although such machines as the Bulldog, Gauntlet and Gladiator were true classics and could perform wonders in the hands of a skilled pilot, they were far behind the monoplane fighters with which Germany was planning to re-equip its clandestine Luftwaffe. The formation of the RAFVR and the Auxiliary Air Force was a bold and imaginative move, and it could be argued that without the personnel that existed within its ranks when war was finally declared, the RAF would have been in a very precarious state. The Auxiliary Air Force was regarded by many as nothing more than a flying club for wealthy young men. It certainly attracted men with a higher social standing than the VR, higher indeed than most of those who had volunteered to serve on the RAF Short Service Commission scheme.

There are many apocryphal stories that are often quoted in support of this view, including outrageous examples of means tests and the ability to consume a large quantity of alcohol yet still retain all the social graces. There is no doubt that most officers of the pre-war AAF squadrons did belong to what was in effect an exclusive club which allowed them to fly very powerful aeroplanes more or less as a hobby at weekends. Nonetheless, when the chips were down they proved to be superlative airmen, in most cases born leaders, but above all more than ready to fight and die for freedom.

On the outbreak of war, 14 AAF squadrons were absorbed into the RAF's Fighter Command, adding much needed strength and experience. It was once said that in terms of the class distinction prevailing in the pre-war RAF, the auxiliaries were gentlemen trying to be officers, the regulars were officers trying to be gentlemen, and the VR was neither trying to be both! Tony Eyre was a typical member of the AAF, and if fate had not taken a hand when he reached the rank of Wing Commander, he would no doubt have joined the group of top-scoring aces who became household names.

Educated at Whitgift School, Croydon, he was commissioned in the AAF in July 1938 when he was just 20 years old. He flew Gladiators with No 615 (County of Surrey) Squadron from Kenley, a far cry from his native Lowestoft, and when war was declared in September 1939 he had accumulated much experience and reached the rank of Flying Officer. No 615 and No 607 (County of Durham) Squadrons were in the process of converting to Hurricanes when they moved to France, and the spring of 1940 saw Eyre still flying the biplane fighter from Vitry-en-Artois when the so-called Phoney War became very real.

His first three victories were scored whilst he was flying the Gladiator, a superb machine with which to take on the Luftwaffe's bombers, but vulnerable to say the least when it came to encountering the Bf 109. Both auxiliary squadrons were evacuated to England as their bases were systematically destroyed by the Luftwaffe and the advancing Wehrmacht. As the whole country held its breath and waited for the invasion, No 615 completed its conversion to Hurricanes and, when the Battle of Britain started, Eyre and his companions, still operating from Kenley, were able to give a good account of themselves.

Eyre was a master of aerobatics and deflection shooting, and during his first combat patrol in a Hurricane on 11 June he damaged a Bf 109, but could only claim a probable as he did not see it crash. His fourth confirmed victory was the Bf 109 of Leutnant Sherer of 1/*JG* 27 on 20 July and this was followed by a Ju 87 of 10/*LG*1 on 14 August. After his seventh victory, a Dornier Do 17 of 9/*KG* 2 on 20 August, he was awarded a DFC. Two more bombers fell to his guns before the end of the month when the squadron was moved to Prestwick to rest.

When the squadron returned to the south in October, the Luftwaffe had changed its targets and tactics, and No 615 had little success since its Hurricanes were now finding it hard to reach the altitude of incoming raids in the time available. In 1941, the RAF went on the offensive and the by now Flt Lt Eyre was among the first to carry out escort duties in his new Mk 11A Hurricane. On 26 February 1941 the squadron's CO, Sqn Ldr Holmwood, was killed in action, and Tony Eyre assumed command of the unit with which he had served since 1938.

No further successes came his way, and in April he and his flight commanders carried out several night interceptions but again without any luck. A posting to a staff position came on 21 April, and like many of his contemporaries this did nothing but frustrate the now deskbound fighter pilot. Constant harassing of senior officers brought its reward, but he had been away from front-line action for ten months when he was appointed Wing Commander, flying at North Weald.

The spring-like weather brought a resumption of the RAF's offensive campaign with bomber and fighter sweeps over occupied Europe. On 8 March 1942, Wing Commander Eyre led his Spitfire wing into action for the first time escorting bombers attacking targets in the Poissey and Lille areas. FW 190s from Abeville together with F type Bf 109s intercepted the fighters, and Eyre's Spitfire was one of three that failed to return. The gloom that descended over the loss of their popular Wing Commander on his first operation was lifted on 10 March when news was received that he had force-landed and was a prisoner of war. For the next three years he was incarcerated in Stalag Luft 111a at Sagan, Silesia. On liberation, he returned to flying with the peacetime RAF but was killed in February 1946 whilst flying a Meteor.

Tony Eyre achieved ace status fairly quickly, but was one of those pilots who did not have the fortune to be in the right place at the right time. If he had been, it is very likely that his confirmed score of nine, which, in fact, was probably ten, would have been higher. There can be little doubt that his leadership earned him the respect of all ranks, and at times his spirit lifted the morale of his squadron when success was all around but seemed to be eluding them. He was a typical example of an ace who contributed a lot to the well-being of his men and his unit, which, at the time he was in action, was just as important as aerial victories.

BRENDAN FINUCANE

(RAF)

S trict discipline is necessary as a firm basis on which to build any efficient fighting force, but sometimes it can be observed too closely and result in disasters that often nonetheless go down in history as epic encounters; the ill-fated charge of the Light Brigade is perhaps a typical example.

At the beginning of the Second World War, the RAF was using outdated formation flying tactics within its fighter squadrons, these concentrating on strict positional placing and forming up in line astern to carry out attacks. The result was that several pilots, some of whom could well have become aces, died without ever seeing the enemy that shot them out of the sky. In June 1940, a young pilot officer flying his first patrol over Dunkirk was so intent on keeping station that he failed to see any enemy aircraft despite the squadron's attempt to intercept a large enemy formation. It would have been so easy for him to have become an early victim of the air war, but happily it was not to be, and within two years he had reached the rank of Wing Commander, scored 32 victories and been awarded a DSO and three DFCs. That man was the greatest Irish ace to come out of the Second War, Brendan 'Paddy' Finucane.

Born in Dublin on 16 October 1920, Brendan was the eldest of five children who, with their mother and father, moved to Richmond, Surrey, in 1936. On leaving school, he took up employment as a clerk but had a strong leaning towards accountancy, and would probably have followed such a career if he had survived the war. His aptitude for mathematics stood him in a good light when, at the age of 17½ in April 1938, he applied to join the RAF on a short service commission as a pilot. Accepted for training, he 'passed out' in August 1939 and became a fighter pilot flying Spitfires with No 65 Sqn from Hornchurch in the summer of 1940. He fought throughout the Battle of Britain, gaining his first confirmed kill on 12 August when he shot down a Bf 109 of 111/*JG* 54 and damaged another, repeating the sequence the next day, this time the victims being aircraft of 111/*JG* 51.

By 18 August, he had flown 52 sorties and like other pilots who had been in the forefront of the fight since the beginning of July, was starting to feel the strain. On 28 August, No 65 was withdrawn to Turnhouse for a rest and it was not until 4 January 1941 that he added to his total with a Bf 110 which he encountered whilst on patrol from Tangmere and shot into the sea off Selsey. Two weeks later, he shared a Ju 88 and on 4 February a Bf 109 fell to his eight Brownings. On 15 April another Bf 109 brought his total to five confirmed and three probables, but his next victim was rather unusual in that it was his own commanding officer! Posted as 'A' Flight commander to No 452 Sqn, a newly formed Australian fighter squadron, he and Sqn Ldr Dutton, the only other pilot on the unit with combat experience, took off in their Spitfires to practise a formation aerobatic display they were to give for a 'Wings for Victory' week. Finucane flew too close to his leader and his propeller carved a section from the tail of Dutton's aircraft. Both men managed to carry out successful forced landings and neither suffered physical injury, although no doubt Finucane's pride was hurt!

July 1941 saw No 452 fully operational and now under the command of Sqn Ldr Bungey, and he, together with Flt Lt 'Bluey' Truscott who commanded 'B' Flight, completed a deadly trio with Finucane. The Irishman had the quiet, deliberate manner and charm that is often a hallmark of his countrymen. He was as eager as the next man to join in mess parties, but drank little and encouraged his pilots to do the same. His leadership was outstanding and the aura which surrounded him affected air and ground crew alike. He was religious and attended Mass regularly, but never forced his beliefs on anyone, although he would discuss them in his quiet, charming lilt with those who wished to do so.

Operating from Kenley, the Australians made their first contact with the enemy on 11 July 1941 when 14 Spitfires tackled Bf 109s over Abbeville, the first victory going to Finucane. By October, he had shot down a further 18 Bf 109s, shared two more, damaged three and recorded two probables. During this period he came close to achieving a unique event, the destruction of his 21st victim on his 21st birthday, but it was not to be, the Bf 109 that brought this landmark falling to his guns just four days before he achieved his majority.

On 13 October, his coolness and flying skill were ably demonstrated when, on returning from a patrol, he and his wing man saw a lone Spitfire being harried by two Bf 109s. The two No 452 Sqn aircraft promptly dispatched the German fighters to a watery end, but before they could climb back to altitude, Finucane noticed splashes of gunfire on the sea. Carefully noting the angle of the splashes, he waited until they drew closer then pulled his Spitfire into a steep turn which caused the following Bf 109 to overshoot what its pilot must have thought was an 'easy' target. Such was his skill and timing, that Finucane's turn placed the enemy aircraft in the centre of his reflector sight; a short burst saw the Bf 109 stagger as if it had hit a solid wall, then dive into the sea. Later the same day, he claimed yet another Bf 109 to complete his tally for 1941. A DSO was added to the three DFCs he had already been awarded.

Promotion to Squadron Leader and command of No 602 Sqn at Kenley came in January 1942, and with it a deep sense of pride and protection towards what he called his 'boys'. He continued to lead by example, which was really the only way he knew, and whilst taking pride in his squadron's achievements, tended to make light of his own. On one occasion, when LAC Jack Firth painted a neat circle of swastikas around the shamrock emblem that he always carried on his Spitfire *Wheezy Anna*, Finucane told him to wash them off as they were too showy.

On 20 February 1942, whilst returning from a sortie, Finucane and his wing man, Plt Off Richard Lewis, were surprised by two FW 190s. Cannon shells from one of the German fighters tore into Finucane's cockpit, causing the only injury he was to receive in combat. Although in pain from his wounds, he ordered Lewis to head for home, but the young Australian disobeyed Finucane – something very few men risked – and protected his tail as the two Spitfires raced for home at sea level. The FW 190s chased them across the Channel; Lewis turned to face the two Germans and placed a burst squarely into the cockpit of the leader, causing him to dive straight into the sea, at which point his companion hurriedly decided to call it a day. Although weak from loss of blood, Finucane managed a good landing at Kenley and was gently lifted from his shattered cockpit and taken to hospital. His wounds healed quickly and his counter-attack was swift. On 13 March, he shot the tail off a FW 190 and followed this with seven more of the same type during the rest of March and April.

What was to be his 32nd and final victory came on 17 May when his accurate marksmanship severed the port wing from yet another FW 190. This victory equalled the score of the legendary 'Sailor' Malan, achieved a year before, and made Finucane the highest-scoring operational ace at that time. It is likely that on 8 June he accounted for another FW 190, but the German pilot managed to find cloud cover after being damaged, and if he crashed it was not witnessed.

At 21, Finucane became the youngest Wing Commander in the RAF and he arrived at Hornchurch on 21 June to lead the four Spitfire squadrons that comprised the 'Hornchurch Wing'. The fight was now being taken to the enemy in strength, with sweeps over occupied France being carried out almost daily. On 17 July 1942, 'Paddy' Finucane was leading his wing on such a sortie when his aircraft was hit by fire from a single machine-gun post manned by just two Germans in the sand dunes near Pointe du Touquet. Rather than crash-land in France, he set course for home accompanied by Plt Off F. A. Aikman, his No 2 on this occasion. It was clear that the Spitfire's engine was overheating, and just ten miles off the French coast Aikman heard his leader call that he was ditching, saw him remove his helmet and lean forward into the cockpit. The Spitfire hit the sea in the approved manner laid down for ditching, but it sank before Finucane could get out; it is possible that the impact rendered him unconscious, but whatever happened there was only a widening oil slick to mark the grave of a respected and well-loved leader.

His skill is probably best summed up in his own words which he often repeated to his pilots: 'The first necessity in combat is to see the other bloke before he sees you – the second is to hit him first time when you fire. You don't get a second chance in this game.' Finucane was a national hero; over 3,000 people attended a Requiem Mass in Westminster Abbey, and a nationwide appeal resulted in the endowment of the Finucane Ward in the Royal Hospital, Richmond. The gentle Irishman would have been proud of this, and his warm smile would no doubt have been just as great when 'Bluey' Truscott renamed his Spitfire *Paddy* in his honour.

IAN GLEED

(RAF)

*F*ifteen Messerschmitt Bf 109s of *JG* 77 lurked up-sun, their pilots intently watching the Italian SM 82 trimotor transports skimming the waves some 20,000 feet below. The trap was set, and the German pilots were soon rewarded. Leutnant Ernst-Wilhelmm Reinhert, who was to achieve 174 victories and survive the war, saw three Spitfires appear as if from nowhere and dive towards the Italian transports; he delayed his dive and was soon congratulating himself on the pause, for following the trio of British fighters were ten more Allied aircraft. Reinhert mistook the second formation for American Mustangs, but they were in fact clipped-wing Mk Vb Spitfires of No 145 Squadron, and the three leading them into the attack were Spitfire IXs of No 92 Squadron led by Flt Lt Neville Duke.

The British fighters were soon engaging the lumbering SM 82s, two of which quickly fell to Duke's guns. Then all hell was let loose as the Bf 109s arrived, Duke saw a Spitfire plunging earthwards and heard the leader of No 145 calling for assistance, but he could not identify his whereabouts and, as was so often the case with such dogfights, the sky suddenly seemed to clear of the turning fighters. The Spitfire that had been seen falling was that of Flt Sgt J. Rostant who baled out when Leutnant Heinz-Edgar Berres (52 kills) set it on fire.

He had been flying wing-man to the leader of the No 145 Sqn Spitfires and, with his tail unprotected, had become a victim of Lt Reinhert. The date was 16 April 1943, and the man who had fallen to the Luftwaffe ace was one of the RAF's most popular characters and himself an ace with 15 kills to his credit, Wing Commander Ian Richard Gleed, known to his friends as 'Widge'. His body was recovered from the wreckage of Spitfire Vb *AB502* which, in addition to carrying his initials 'IR – G' in place of the standard squadron codes, a privilege extended to wing leaders, also had his 'Figaro' cat insignia painted on the starboard side below the windscreen. The latter is now in the RAF Museum at Hendon together with similar panels from the Hurricanes he flew whilst with No 87 Sqn.

Ian Gleed was the son of a London doctor but, unlike his sister who followed in her father's footsteps, he had no real desire to seek a medical career, and in his final term at Epsom College volunteered and was accepted for a short service commission in the RAF. The 20-year-old pilot officer completed his basic flying training at No 8 FTS and received his 'wings' on Christmas Day 1936 together with the rare distinction of being graded 'exceptional' as a fighter pilot.

His first squadron was No 46 and he spent the next two years happily flying Gladiators from Kenley, obtaining top gradings in navigation and gunnery. By the time war was declared the unit had re-equipped with Hurricanes, but before he could see any action Gleed was posted with the acting rank of Flight Lieutenant to command 'B' Flight of No 226 Sqn. This move could well have been fatal, for on 19 February 1940 the Spitfire he was flying *(N3120)* suffered serious icing and broke up. Gleed was thrown from the cockpit and received serious head and leg injuries, but managed to open his parachute and make a safe descent although his injuries kept him grounded until early May. His career then followed a pattern similar to many of his contemporaries, with a short stay in France with No 87 Sqn, during which, on his first combat patrol on 18 May, he destroyed two Bf 110s. The following day he added a Heinkel He 111, a Dornier Do 17 and a Bf 109, then on his third day in action he shared a Ju 88 with Plt Off Tait and strafed German tanks before returning to North Weald in the evening, as French airfields had become untenable.

The remnants of No 87 gradually gathered at Debden before moving on to Church Fenton to reform with new pilots replacing those lost in the debacle of France. The unit became operational again at Exeter, and on 15 August 'Widge' Gleed recorded his first victories in the Battle of Britain with a pair of Bf 110s and a damaged Bf 109. All these were achieved whilst flying Hurricane *P2798*, an aircraft which had arrived in France on 17 May straight from the MU and had been adopted by Gleed as his personal machine. Coded *LK-A*, it was the first of his fighters to carry the Walt Disney 'Figaro' cat insignia.

The well-deserved award of a DFC came in September, by which time No 87 had already started to experiment with night patrols and intruder sorties. On 12 December, Gleed flew his first night sortie over occupied France, returning empty handed but on Christmas Eve he received two early presents: promotion to Squadron Leader and command of No 87. Intruder missions continued whenever weather permitted, and Gleed was successful in destroying several enemy aircraft on the ground, although these did not of course count towards his final score.

His next aerial kill occurred on 7 May when he shot a Do 17 into the Channel. Later that month he was in the rather enviable position of operating from the Scilly Isles, and on the 24th had a most unusual victory over either a very brave or very unwise Luftwaffe pilot. Gleed, on this occasion flying Hurricane *W9196*, was returning to St Mary's with his No 2, Sgt Thorogood, and was about to land, when a Dornier Do 18 flying boat appeared from cloud and *attacked* the two British fighters. Overcoming his surprise at this audacity, Gleed promptly retracted his undercarriage and flaps, pulled the Hurricane into a steep turn and at maximum deflection shot the Do 18 into the sea with one burst.

A damaged Ju 88 on 28 May was his last victory of 1941; further promotion came in November together with a move to Middle Wallop, and then on to Ibsley to command the wing in 1942. Strangely enough, he re-opened his account where he left off with a Ju 88 falling to his Spitfire on 22 March. The award of a DSO followed in May, and after two years of almost continuous operational flying he was ordered to rest.

The following year started with the rejuvenated Wing Commander shaking off the shackles of his chairborne tour and reporting to HQ Middle East Air Force to become wing leader of No 244 Wing, 211 Group, of the Northern Area Tactical Air Force, his command comprising Nos 92, 145, 417, 601 and 1 Sqn SAAF. On 7 March, flying his personal Spitfire *AB502*, he destroyed a Bf 109G, and on the 17th, whilst returning from a commanders' conference, bagged another.

On 16 April, he took off at 14.10 from Goubrina to patrol the Cap Bon area looking for transport aircraft taking supplies to the Afrika Korps. The ten Spitfires he was leading had three from No 92 as top cover. An hour later, *JG* 77 sprung their trap . . .

In addition to his British decorations, Wing Commander Gleed was also awarded the Belgian *Croix de Guerre*, and posthumously, on 5 June 1946, the French *Croix de Guerre avec Etoile Vermeil*.

COLIN GRAY

(RAF)

*D*etermination is something that has carried many an achiever to the top of his chosen profession, and can be traced as one of the major factors common to the careers of many aces. The career of Colin Gray, one of twin boys born on 9 November 1914 in Papanui, New Zealand, illustrates the point admirably.

As a youngster he suffered from pleurisy, osteomyelitis and conjunctivitis, it was not surprising therefore that he failed his medical when, with his twin brother Kenneth, he volunteered to join the RAF on a short service commission in 1936. Ken was, however, accepted, and departed for England in 1937 where he went to the civil flying college at Desford to start his initial flying training. Meanwhile, Colin became more determined to follow in his brother's footsteps and re-applied to the RAF in 1937, only to be rejected again. Lesser men may well have called it a day, but Colin was far from being beaten. In 1938, he once again presented himself in Wellington and this time passed the aircrew medical and on 18 December 1938 set sail for England aboard RMS *Rangitata*, arriving in London one month later. By this time, his brother had gained his 'wings' and was with No 102 Sqn at Driffield where, on 12 December 1938 (six days before Colin sailed from New Zealand), he qualified as a 1st pilot on Whitleys.

Five days after arriving in England, Colin started his flying training at Hatfield with No 1 EFTS, and on 1 April 1939 was commissioned as an Acting Pilot Officer and moved on to No 11 FTS where he flew Harts, Hinds and Audaxes. He graduated to Harvards at St Athan then, unlike his brother who had followed a similar pattern up to this point, he converted to Hurricanes instead of twins and the die was cast for him to become a fighter pilot. However, his career in this capacity nearly ended before it began. Posted to No 54 Sqn at Hornchurch, his arrival on 20 November could hardly have been less sensational; as he levelled out for what he hoped would be a perfect three-point landing, he failed to notice a sandbagged air raid shelter near the perimeter. The Spitfire juddered as its main undercarriage was torn off, and the embarrassed pilot completed a belly landing which was witnessed not only by the station commander and his squadron CO but also the AOC-in-C Fighter Command, Sir Hugh Dowding, who expressed his puzzlement to the gathered officers by remarking 'I could have sworn that Spitfire had his wheels down'.

Plt Off Gray was taken before the station commander who threatened to have him posted from a Spitfire squadron to target-towing duties at a gunnery school, but fortunately 54's CO Sqn Ldr H. M. Pearson, spoke up for the young pilot and persuaded officialdom to let him stay with the squadron. This was a decision that was to cost the Luftwaffe dearly, and lead to Colin Gray becoming New Zealand's highest-scoring and most decorated fighter pilot.

Apart from a few inconclusive patrols and scrambles, No 54 saw no action until May, but meanwhile Colin's brother had been making the Gray presence felt among the enemy with bombing and leaflet raids over enemy territory. It was on returning from a raid on 27 November that Ken's Whitley was seriously damaged by lightning. He and his crew managed to get the aircraft back to England where Gray and his second pilot, Plt Off Frank Long, received immediate awards of the DFC.

On 7 May, Ken Gray took off from Kinloss to fly to Driffield where he had arranged to spend some leave with his fighter-pilot brother, but *en route* the Whitley encountered bad weather and flew into a hill near Dyce. The rear gunner was the sole survivor. Flying Officer Ken Gray was buried in the churchyard at Dyce, and nine days later Colin had his first opportunity to uphold his brother's honour when he flew his first operational sortie over Calais, Ostend and Dunkirk, but it was not until 24 May that he recorded his first claim when he damaged a Bf 109 over Calais.

The following day, soon after sharing a Bf 109 with Sgt Norwell, he was hit by cannon fire from another Bf 109 which caused him to hurry away to Hornchurch where, with no brakes or flaps, and having to pump his wheels down by hand, he made a successful forced landing. A short rest at Catterick delayed his first solo claim which was achieved on 13 July when he shot down Ltn Lange of 111/*JG* 51. Eleven days later he fought a pair of Bf 109s, sending one spinning down seemingly out of control, but Gray could not watch to see if it hit the ground as its companion, flown by Ltn Schauf of 111/*JG* 26, was taking all his attention. The New Zealander had to call on all his skill to outwit the German, but eventually he found the opening he sought, fired a burst from his guns and saw flames belch from the German fighter. Eight miles east of Margate, the German took to his parachute and fell into the Channel; this time there was no doubt about the outcome, so a victory was credited to the 54 Squadron pilot.

In August, Gray shot down six more Bf 109s including two during one sortie on 12 August. He also proved his prowess against the heavily armed but far less manoeuvrable Bf 110 with a probable on 16 August, and two confirmed and a damaged on 18th. The award of a DFC came in August, and his score continued to mount with the first three days of September seeing his contribution to the conclusion of the Battle of Britain. The 2nd was his busiest day of the Battle, with five sorties which brought him another Bf 109 and a Bf 110 in between which the Luftwaffe went part of the way to levelling the score when a Bf 109 damaged his Spitfire, forcing another emergency landing at Hornchurch. The following day, No 54 was withdrawn to Catterick. Gray was one of only five of the original 17 pilots left flying with the unit, and his score of 16 confirmed plus eight probables and shared kills put him among the top fighter pilots of the Battle.

In December, Gray was promoted to Flight Lieutenant and given command of 'A' Flight. No 54 returned to Hornchurch with Spitfire IIAs on 23 February 1941, then in June Gray moved to No 1 Sqn, flying Hurricanes from Redhill. Success with this new type was almost immediate, as together with his wing-man he shot down a Heinkel 59 off Folkestone on 16 June. His 17th confirmed victory came on 22 August when he was flying with No 41 Sqn and shot down a Bf 109F over Le Havre. One month later came the award of a Bar to his DFC, promotion to Squadron Leader and command of No 403 Sqn.

The latter lasted only two days, for on 1 October he was ordered to report to Tangmere to take over the reins of No 616 Sqn. He followed the life of a nomad for a few months before being taken off operations for a staff job at No 9 Group HQ. Returning to combat in September 1942, he flew escort and fighter sweeps with Nos 485 and 64 Sqns before taking command of 81 Sqn in Algiers in January 1943. He soon showed that the rest had not affected his flying or gunnery and, now at the controls of a Mk IX Spitfire, he was soon adding the latest 'G' versions of the Bf 109 to his tally.

There were many occasions when he damaged enemy aircraft, but, like many other aces, he allowed less experienced pilots of the squadron to administer the *coupe de grâce* to help their confidence. On 23 April his patience must have been tried when, after shooting down a Bf 109, his wing-man claimed the kill; Gray's comments when it was found that the pilot in question had not fired his guns are not recorded.

On 15 May 1943 he was awarded the DSO, and 4 June was promoted to Wing Commander with command of No 322 Wing. His command was very much involved in the invasion of Sicily, and the Wing moved to the island on 22 July. During this period, Gray added a Maachi 202 to the types of enemy aircraft he had shot down in combat, and just for good measure included three Ju 52s, a trio from a total of 26 destroyed by the Wing in one sortie when they massacred the German transport aircraft on 25 July.

These lumbering giants proved to be his last victories, for in September he completed his second tour of ops and returned to England where in November he received a Bar to his DSO. More staff jobs followed, but he ended the war once again in the hot seat as OC Flying at Detling, and Wing Commander Flying at Lympne, where he flew Spitfire XIVs on patrols and anti-V1 (Diver) sorties. His third operational tour ended on VE Day, 8 May 1945, by which time he had accumulated over 630 hours operational flying and was officially credited with 28 victories. He served with the peace-time RAF until 1961 when he retired to return to his native New Zealand.

JAMES LACEY

(RAF)

The pilot of Hurricane *P2793* peered through the windscreen into the swirling cloud that surrounded his aircraft. He listened intently as the Ground Controller guided him eastwards, then south, then east, then south-east, but still there was no sign of the enemy bomber he had volunteered to try to find in the solid cloud that covered the south of England. It was 13 September 1940, at the height of what was to become known as the Battle of Britain, and that morning the Hurricane pilot had returned to 501 Sqn at Kenley from a short spell of leave.

A fifty-minute patrol by the squadron in the fine weather of the early morning had produced no results, then just as the pilots were looking forward to lunch and a break from flying as the cloud cover spread, Sector Ops had asked for a volunteer to take off in the murky conditions to look for a bomber that was somewhere over London. Breaking cloud at 14,000 feet, the sergeant pilot suddenly caught a glimpse of the bomber as it momentarily slipped out of the cloud. The lightning reactions that had already earned him a DFM with five victories in France and eleven so far in the Battle were still honed to perfection despite the break from action, and almost automatically he threw his fighter into a dive, at the same time firing a short but lethal burst from his eight Brownings, killing the bomber's rear gunner.

The enemy aircraft was a Heinkel He 111 of 111/*KG* 27 flown by Oblt Harry Wappler, and he immediately took evasive action, believing that he had shaken off the British fighter in the darkness of the cloud. But he had not reckoned with the tenacity of the Hurricane's 23-year-old pilot, who had sensed the Heinkel's every move and now sat slightly below and to one side of it instead of squarely on its tail. It had been a masterful piece of flying, since most of the time he could only see a shadowy shape as the German pilot twisted and turned to shake off his tormentor. Satisfied that the British plane had gone, the German climbed through the cloud and turned for home. The Hurricane closed in for the kill, but the Germans were a long way from being finished. Knowing that they might not be entirely safe, another crew member had taken the place of the dead gunner, and as both aircraft broke into sunlight the German saw the Hurricane, fired at it and recorded hits in the radiator and engine. Simultaneously, the British pilot also opened fire and soon both aircraft were blazing, the

Hurricane from its coolant tank and the Heinkel from both engines. The sergeant pulled back his canopy and baled out of the stricken fighter, whilst the Heinkel took Wappler and the rest of its crew to a fiery end in a Kentish field.

A typical story from the tense days of 1940? Perhaps, but one with a lasting difference, for the Heinkel had just bombed Buckingham Palace and the Hurricane's young pilot was Sgt James 'Ginger' Lacey who, with 18 victories, was the RAF's top scoring ace in the Battle of Britain.

Few people realise that nearly half (44 per cent) of the RAF's aircrew who fought in the Battle of Britain were NCOs, a good proportion of whom were young men like Geoffrey Allard and Frank Carey who had joined the Service as Apprentices, served in the very junior ranks and crossed the far from easy hurdle of qualifying as sergeant pilots in the peacetime RAF. Others had followed the same path as 'Ginger' Lacey, a routine civilian job broken at weekends by the thrill of learning to fly, then serving in the RAF Volunteer Reserve. Such men had for many reasons either been unable or not entirely willing to enlist in the full-time RAF, but wanted to fly or 'do their bit' for their country. In the days when the RAF was expanding to meet the sinister threat that had been building up on the continent, the dedication of such men was acknowledged by politicians, who had a clear understanding of what was happening, and the public, which was becoming more and more aware that some form of strong air defence was long overdue.

Even so, it was still touch-and-go when the Battle of Britain was at its zenith and, if it had not been for men like Lacey and those who had followed a similar but commissioned path in the Auxiliary Air Force, the shortage of trained pilots may well have brought the defeat that at one stage looked very likely.

James Lacey was the son of a Yorkshireman whose roots were deep in the soil of his native county. When James left school, he stated that he would like to become an RAF Apprentice, but his father was not convinced that this was a path to prosperity. So James listened to his father's advice and, although perhaps not entirely agreeing with it, eventually respected his wishes and fully intended to take up farming. However, he changed his mind, and with several good School Certificate passes to his credit including chemistry, he turned towards pharmacy, but part of him still resolved to fly. The determination that is a characteristic of most Yorkshiremen eventually took him through the entry interview and medical for the RAFVR and he reported to Stone in Scotland where he became the first of his intake of 30 to fly solo.

Lacey proved to be a natural pilot and became an instructor at the Yorkshire Aeroplane Club. On mobilization, he was posted to No 501 Sqn and headed for France in May 1940. On the 13th he scored his first victory, a Bf 109, which was followed by a He 111 and a Bf 110 later the same day. Two more He 111s on the 27th brought him 'ace' status before his return to England, but 9 June might well have brought the end of the Lacey story, for on that day he made an emergency landing and was nearly drowned when his Hurricane turned over in a swamp. Happily, he was rescued in the nick of time and went on to reach new heights.

By the end of October 1940, his score stood at 23 and he had been shot down and forced to bale out on nine occasions, but, unlike the feline family, that was not the end of the road. Lacey was awarded a Bar to his DFM in December and was commissioned the same month. In 1941, he converted to Spitfires, became a Flight Commander and added more victories to his tally before becoming an instructor at No 57 OTU. Later he served with No 602 Sqn, then became Tactics Officer at HQ 81 Group.

In March 1943 he went to India, where he flew Hurricanes and P-47s, became Tactics Officer to 3 Tactical Air Command, went on an Air Fighting Instructors' course where he met Frank Carey, then, in November 1944, took command of No 155 Squadron and later No 17 in Burma. On 19 February 1945 he added a Nakajima Ki 43 to his score-sheet, but this was to be his 28th and last victory. He became the first RAF pilot to fly a Spitfire over Japan on 30 April 1946, then his post-war career continued on Vampires and Hunters before he became a Fighter Controller. On leaving the RAF, he continued to fly at the Yorkshire Flying Club and with Air Experience Flights giving ATC cadets their first taste of flying.

In 1983 he was one of a handful of former Battle of Britain fighter pilots who attended the International Air Tattoo's Tribute to Sir Douglas Bader at RAF Greenham Common. One of the pre-show promotions was a competition organized by a local paper, and the winner was to attend the show as a guest, meet the pilots and receive a painting of a Spitfire signed by the veterans. The winner and his family arrived early, and as they stood waiting to be introduced to the personalities, the winner said, 'What I am really looking forward to is meeting "Ginger" Lacey . . . he's the pilot who shot down the Heinkel that bombed Buckingham Palace, you know.'

Some 43 years after the event, his prowess on that murky September afternoon was still being recalled with pride by a member of the public who placed it above all the remarkable collective achievements of the rather select band gathered at Greenham Common on that day.

JOHANNES LEROUX

(RAF)

On 16 July 1944, both German land and air forces were under pressure as the Allies capitalized on the air superiority that had given them a tremendous edge during the June invasion. The Luftwaffe, however, was still far from beaten, and although initially their fighters, now mainly FW 190s, were not plentiful, they were more than capable of giving a good account of themselves both in air-to-air combat and, if successful in eluding the Allied fighter umbrella, in strafing troops and transport on the ground.

Allied pilots were also keen to 'mix it' at all levels, and although some fighter pilots did not like going too near the ground, especially in aircraft like the Spitfire that was not primarily designed for the ground attack role, they did seek targets of opportunity. On the day in question, No 602 Sqn, which had moved with its Mk Vb and IX Spitfires to France on 25 June, was briefed to carry out an armed reconnaissance in the battle area near Fleurs. They bounced six Bf 109s and the leader soon sent one spinning to the ground; engaging a second, he saw hits on the enemy aircraft, then noticed a German staff car complete with motorcycle outrider weaving a solitary path along the narrow roads below.

The Spitfire pilot pulled his aircraft into a wing-over and screamed into the attack, a wry grin spreading across his face as he saw the car weaving to avoid his fire, then crashing into the ditch. He pulled his aircraft into a climb and rejoined his companions before heading for home. The man in the staff car had been Field Marshal Erwin Rommel, and his injuries were such that he had to be replaced as commander of the German forces on the Western Front. The pilot who had unwittingly come so close to killing the great German soldier was a South African with a German-sounding first name and a French-sounding surname, Sqn Ldr Johannes LeRoux, already an ace and equally at home whether attacking air or ground targets.

'Chris', as he was known to his friends, followed a similar path to that trodden by many South Africans and others from many nations, by volunteering for service with the RAF just before the outbreak of war. He had a very dramatic start to his career as a fighter pilot with No 73 Sqn during operations in France in 1940, being shot down 12 times without recording one victory. So, when he joined No 91 Sqn in 1941 he had a lot of leeway to make up, and was very keen to redress the balance. He did not have too long to wait, for on 17 August 1941 his squadron was ordered to intercept enemy aircraft that were escorting a tanker east of Calais. Five aircraft from No 91 led by Flg Off Paddy Barthropp joined forces with aircraft from No 72 and were soon in combat with approximately 20 Bf 109s. Barthropp, Plt Off Donahue and LeRoux all sent German fighters to watery graves, so at last the South African had struck back.

The nature of the patrol work upon which he was engaged took LeRoux on low-level sweeps over the Channel and occupied France, so he quickly became accustomed to strafing anything he saw whilst over enemy territory. An early example of this came in late August when on the 26th he destroyed four Bf 109s on the airfield at Furnes/Coxyde, on the 29th a Bf 109 in the air near Calais, and on the following day supply barges off the same port.

LeRoux had lightning reactions and was never a man to take unnecessary chances; this was well illustrated by an action on 30 October when, as he crossed the French coast, he encountered heavy and accurate antiaircraft fire. Deciding that discretion was the better part of valour, he headed back out to sea where he attacked two flak-ships. Five days later he showed he had no preference for any type of target by first fighting an inconclusive combat with an FW 190, then shooting at soldiers and lorries and, on the way home, strafing a ship nestling in Boulogne harbour!

By this time he had already received several congratulatory letters from his AOC as well as collecting a DFC on 4 October. His first tour ended in December, but he returned to No 91 as a flight commander the following autumn. On 31 October he shot down a pair of FW 190s that had bombed Canterbury, and this brought him another 'well done' letter from his AOC. In January he was posted to No 111 Sqn and moved to Algiers, where on the 19th he opened his North African account. This tour continued successfully until April when he returned to England, was given command of No 602 Sqn and began his third operational tour on 8 July 1944. His first sortie on 12 July brought no aerial combat, but a blazing three-ton truck showed that he had not lost his touch or appetite for ground targets.

His final victory came on 20 July when he shared a FW 190 with Flg Off Oliver, the remainder of the month being occupied with ground attack work. By now he had received two Bars to his original DFC and was once again 'rested' from ops. As is often the case, fate now took a hand and on 19 September 1944 this talented and popular South African was killed in an accident. He is officially credited with 22½ victories, of which 16½ were enemy aircraft destroyed in air-to-air combat. As well as these, there are countless trucks, small ships and, of course, Rommel's staff car.

ADOLF MALAN

(RAF)

*T*here are many examples of those who have seen the horrors of war at first hand subsequently turning their hands and hearts to helping the less fortunate. It is not a question of easing a troubled conscience, or any other moral or religious reason although perhaps in some cases such reasons do have some part to play. It is more often the in-born leadership that has taken them to the front in combat seeking a new challenge, and adding the weight of the fame their name has brought to the sterling work carried out in such areas by legions of dedicated workers. The names of Leonard Cheshire and Douglas Bader, the former with the Cheshire Homes and the latter with the Bader Foundation and Flying Scholarships for the disabled, come readily to mind in England; in much-troubled South Africa, when the question turns to the much vexed subject of apartheid, the name of Adolf Malan will soon come into the conversation.

Malan, or 'Sailor' as he was generally known, left the RAF in 1946 after a distinguished career as a fighter pilot and, before his early death from Parkinson's disease in September 1963, became National President of 'Torch Command', the ex-servicemen's anti-apartheid movement. He much preferred to be known for the work he carried out on behalf of this organization than the estimated 34 victories that at one time placed him as the top-scoring Allied ace of the Second World War.

Malan was a South African by birth, and turned to the sea for his living, carrying out his early training on the *General Botha* training ship before becoming an officer in the Merchant Navy. At 25 he decided to seek further adventure and turned from the sea to the sky, enlisting in the then expanding Royal Air Force in 1935 and becoming a fighter pilot with No 74 Sqn flying Gauntlets. By 1938, Malan was a flight commander and demonstrated his natural flair for leadership by guiding his flight to victory in that year's Sir Phillip Sassoon Trophy.

Malan's first taste of action came over the beaches of Dunkirk in May 1940, and within a week he had achieved 'ace' status with five confirmed and two probables to his credit, which also brought the award of a DFC in June. His all-round skill as a fighter pilot was ably demonstrated on the night of 19 June 1940, when he took off in his Spitfire to try to intercept German night raiders. The Spitfire was far from ideal as a night fighter, but

Wing Commander Colin Grey DSO DFC, OC No 322 Wing, on 7 August 1943 (via Chaz Bowyer).

Left *The Spitfire VB of Wing Commander Ian 'Widge' Gleed DSO DFC. It carries his initials in place of the squadron codes.* (via Norman Franks).

Below left *Gleed in the cockpit of his Spitfire VB, showing his Figaro mascot and rank pennant* (via Norman Franks).

Right *Gleed poses by his Spitfire* (via Chaz Bowyer, copyright Dr D. I. L. Gleed).

Below *Sqn Ldr Johannes J. 'Chris' Le Roux, a South African who during 1940 was shot down 12 times. He was killed in an accident on 19 September 1944* (via Norman Franks).

Above far left *Sqn Ldr James 'Ginger' Lacey who, as a Sgt Pilot, was one of the leading aces during the Battle of Britain* (via Norman Franks).

Above left *Famous for his 'Rules of Air Fighting', the much respected Group Captain Adolph Malan* (via Chaz Bowyer).

Left *A trio of aces, Malan, Charles and Deere, at Biggin Hill in 1943* (via Norman Franks).

Above *Generally believed to be the RAF's top-scoring ace of the Second World War, Sqn Ldr M. T. St J. Pattle DFC*, killed in action over Athens on 20 April 1941* (via Chaz Bowyer).

Above right *Flt Lt Willie Rhodes-Moorhouse DFC, whose father won the Victoria Cross in the First World War* (via Chaz Bowyer).

Right *Wing Commander Stanislaw Skalski, who returned to Poland after the war and became a taxi driver* (Via Norman Franks).

Above *Sqn Ldr Richard Playne Stevens DSO DFC, the highest-scoring Hurricane night fighter pilot* (drawing by Eric Kennington).

Below *A nap hand of American aces: (l–r) Gabreski, Cook, Johnson, Schilling, Mahurin and Landry, photographed in 1944* (via Chaz Bowyer).

Above *Major Walter Dhal in the cockpit of his Bf 109 on the Eastern Front* (Author's collection).

Below *Adolf Galland taxis his Bf 109E-4 to its dispersal in France on 23 August 1940 after a sortie over England during the Battle of Britain* (Author's collection).

Above *Major Erich Hartmann (right) at Waffenschule 10 Oldenburg in 1958, before the WGAF officers were allowed to wear their Second World War decorations. Sqn Ldr D. Warren RCAF, pictured with Hartmann, said that he felt rather foolish wearing his alongside the German ace of aces (via Chaz Bowyer).*

Below *Reich Marschall Hermann Göring with Hpt z Lippe Weisenfeldt, Major Hermann Lent, an unknown officer and Hpt Manfred Meurer (via Chaz Bowyer).*

Malan was such a master of his machine that he was able to fly it by instinct while searching the moonlit skies. His vigilance was rewarded, and he accounted for a pair of Heinkel He 111s within a 20-minute period before executing a perfect touch-down in the dark, no mean feat bearing in mind the narrow track of the Spitfire's undercarriage. These two night victories brought him an immediate Bar to his DFC.

In July, the Battle of Britain started in earnest, and on the 12th he shared a He 111 of 11/*KG* 53 with Plt Off Stevenson and Sgt Mould, a week later accounting for a Bf 109 of 11/*JG* 51. On 28 July he was engaged in combat with a Bf 109, the pilot of which nearly proved his match, but eventually the Spitfire pilot managed to get the upper hand and claimed a probable as the German fighter departed in a hurry towards France. It was later discovered that this Bf 109E-3 was being flown by Maj Werner Moelders, the *Geschwader Kommander* of *JG* 51 who was to become the first Luftwaffe pilot to score 100 victories and whose total stood at 115 when he was killed in a flying accident in November 1941.

Two more 109s and a couple of Do 17s in August completed his tally for the Battle of Britain; during August, No 74, commanded by the now Sqn Ldr Malan, was moved for a rest to Kirton-in-Lindsey where he wrote his famous '10 Rules of Air Fighting', a document that was circulated throughout the RAF and was still to be seen in some fighter pilots' crew rooms in Korea in the early 1950s when jets were engaged in aerial combat with each other for the first time.

No 74 returned to the south during the autumn and Malan led it into action from Biggin Hill, initially against high-level and low-level hit-and-run raiders, then in excursions across the Channel. By the end of 1940, his score stood at 18 and he was leading the Biggin Hill Wing. As the RAF carried the offensive to occupied Europe, Malan's wing was occupied with escort duties and there were few chances of increasing personal scores, but in June the tempo increased and in just over a month he had accounted for 14 Bf 109s, his final kill of the war being achieved on 4 July 1941. At that time his total of 32 made him the top-scoring Allied ace, and, by the time damaged and shared aircraft were taken into account, his final tally could well have been the 35 claimed in his biography.

In October he went to the USA on a goodwill mission, and whilst there gave many lectures and occasionally flew with instructors and pupils of the US Army Air Corps. On one such occasion he 'destroyed' 12 P 39 fighters with his camera gun in the space of just under 5 minutes! Returning to England, he instructed at the Central Gunnery School, Sutton Bridge, before being promoted to Group Captain and returning to Biggin Hill as station commander in January 1943. At the time of the Normandy Invasion in June 1944 he was commanding No 20 Fighter Wing and flew several sorties over the beach-heads. The following month he took over as commander of the Advanced Gunnery School, where he had five aces, including 'Screwball' Beurling, serving under him as instructors, a formidable line-up that must have imparted a great deal of confidence to the students.

Despite attending a Staff College course in 1945 which seemed to bode well for his future in the post-war RAF, he decided against a peacetime service career and returned to South Africa in 1946, becoming secretary to Harry Oppenheimer before, in 1950, starting his own sheep farm at Kimberley. His interest in 'Torch Command' gradually took more and more of his time, and he was not just an 'on paper' activist. Deteriorating health took its toll, but he put up a brave fight as one would expect from a man of such undoubted courage, but in the end lost his fight against the final enemy and died at the early age of 53.

THOMAS ST JOHN PATTLE

(RAF)

*G*eneralization can be nearly as dangerous as speculation, but it is interesting to see how the backgrounds of many aces are similar in several ways, and how many of the youthful attributes identified have contributed to success in flying and fighting in aeroplanes. Apart from a wide variety of academic standards, there are often very early examples of sport or adventure activities that have required lightning co-ordination of hand and eye, or others demanding a degree of self-confidence and assurance. Marmaduke Thomas St John Pattle, to give him his full name, fits this description admirably.

Born in Butterworth, Cape Province, South Africa, on 23 July 1914, 'Pat', as he was more commonly known to his friends, spent a great deal of his leisure time with his elder brother Cecil camping and hunting in the wild rugged country that surrounded their home. The family had a military background, and his father's knowledge of guns and shooting was absorbed by young Pat who quickly proved to have a sharp eye and unerring marksmanship. He was also a very accomplished mathematician and a competent self-taught mechanic who at the age of 12 had dismantled the engine of his father's Ford and persuaded it to spring into life when efforts by more competent people had failed. Not content with this, he then drove the car to his father's office where a surprised Pattle senior treated his young son to lunch. No doubt he had a few harsh words to say about the legality of his son's actions and apparent lack of consideration for the law in the privacy of the family home!

Like many youngsters of the period, Pattle was enthralled by stories of aerial combat from the Great War and his major ambition was to become a pilot. In 1933 he applied to join the South African Air Force which at that time was extremely selective, and was disappointed when he failed to be one of the three chosen from his entry of 33. However, recalling the Pattle family motto 'Perseverance' he vowed not to give up until he wore the coveted pilot's wings.

Pattle worked in the mining industry until 1936 when he surrendered a well-paid job to join the Special Service Battalion in South Africa with a view to using this as a means of eventually entering the Air Force. Then, in March 1936 he learned of the RAF's expansion programme and its short-service commission scheme. He immediately applied, was accepted for training as a pilot and started his training at Prestwick on 29 June 1936.

The South African proved to be a natural pilot and graduated with honours in the top three of his class. He joined No 80 Squadron as a pilot officer in 1937 and in 1938, with the international situation deteriorating, moved to Egypt with No 80 to strengthen the RAF's presence in the Suez Canal Zone. When war was declared, Pattle was a flight commander and was as anxious as the rest of the squadron to become involved in the action. Tales of activities in Norway and France only served to frustrate the pilots of No 80 who were then flying routine patrols in their obsolescent Gladiator biplane fighters.

In June 1940, when it seemed that it was only a question of time before Germany won the war, Italy declared war on the Allies, and the Middle East squadrons were soon in action. Initially, No 33 was in the forefront, but, when a flight commander was injured, Pattle was detached to replace him. However, although he was involved in several scrambles and escort patrols including attempts to intercept night raids, the contact he longed for with the enemy did not materialize and he became more and more despondent. Hurricanes had started to replace the nimble but ageing Gladiators, but 'Pat' hankered after the biplane perhaps because he, like many pilots with a similar background, found it a superb aerobatic machine and no doubt, if the truth were known, more akin to the type of aircraft flown by their heroes of the 1914-18 war.

On Sunday 4 August 1940, 'B' Flight was ordered to escort a No 208 Sqn Lysander which had been detailed to reconnoitre enemy troop movements in the Bir Taieb el Esem area. Pattle took three other Gladiators with him, flown by Flg Offs Wykeham-Barnes and Johnny Lancaster, and Sgt Rew. Whilst over enemy territory, the Gladiator pilots saw the Lysander crew fire a Very cartridge indicating they were being attacked. Despite the hawk-like vision of the fighter pilots, they had failed to notice the arrival of Italian fighters that had been escorting Breda 65 light bombers. Diving towards their charge, the RAF aircraft were soon in the thick of a dangerous aerial ballet with the Italians, proving their mastery of the skills of aerobatics.

Pattle had his work cut out to avoid the Italian CR 32 and 42 fighters, and soon lost sight of his companions, but in a gut-wrenching turning circle he noticed an Italian and a Gladiator spinning earthwards, both emitting smoke. His determination took on a new dimension and soon one of a pair of Bredas that were trying to avoid combat by dropping their small 20 lb bombs and diving towards safety was momentarily in his gun sight, but long enough for the South African to fire a short burst at full deflection. Hits on the Italian aircraft slowed it, and, avoiding the attention of the escorting fighters, Pattle caught up with it and a well-aimed burst from his Brownings recorded his first victory.

However, his triumph was short-lived for as he attempted to regain height he was bounced by twelve CR 42s. In the following combat he downed one of the Italians but sheer numbers overwhelmed him and as he turned to avoid the fire from one he flew straight into the sights of another. The Italian made no mistake, and soon Pattle's Gladiator was seriously damaged with the rudder controls virtually shot away. Climbing to 400 feet he abandoned the stricken machine and, although he was on the low side for total safety, his parachute opened just in time and he suffered no more than bruising when he landed. Pattle realised that he was behind enemy lines, and his survival kit, which included a two-gallon tank of water under his seat, was now lost in the blazing wreck of his aircraft.

The time was 19.15, so after burying his parachute he waited until darkness then set off in the direction of Sidi Barrani. He walked through the night, resting frequently, then when the sun started to rise was horrified to discover that he had been walking away from friendly territory. During the following day he was twice nearly caught by Italian patrols but hid in the sand-dunes and the next night set off again. He crossed into friendly territory without realising it and was at the point of total exhaustion when he was discovered by a patrol from the 11th Hussars which took him back to the base from where he had taken off 48 hours before. The twist in the tale that Pattle never lived down was that 'city gent' Wykeham-Barnes, who had also been shot down but had no experience of living rough as Pattle had when he explored the veldt with his brother, had managed to return to base in record time without getting lost. Nonetheless, Pattle's marksmanship and the outdoor activities of his youth had gained him two aerial victories and saved his life.

His total was doubled four days later when he accounted for a pair of CR 42s, and from then on he scored regularly. In November the squadron moved to Greece where he was immediately in the thick of the fighting. In December he was awarded a DFC which he celebrated on the 20th by accounting for a SM 79 and a SM 81. The New Year was only 28 days old when a Cant Z 1007 fell to his guns, and by 10 February his total stood in excess of 27 when he at last swopped his Gladiator for a Hurricane. Unfortunately, records covering the Greek campaign are incomplete and it is impossible to tell exactly how many combats or victories Pattle and his squadron achieved. His last flight was on 20 April, by which time the continuous fighting to cover the Allied withdrawal from the islands had taken its toll.

He was tired and suffering from a bout of influenza when he took off from Eleusis near Athens to intercept a German raid. During the ensuing combat he shot down two Bf 110s and probably a Bf 109 before being seen to go to help one of his flight commanders, W. J. Woods, who was being harassed by two Bf 110s. Pattle failed to notice two more German fighters that came out of the sun on to his uncovered tail. He was last seen slumped over the controls of his Hurricane as it dived into the waters of Eleusis Bay.

His official score was put at over 40, but veterans of the Greek campaign claim that it was probably nearer 60, and it is very likely that this small dynamic South African who won two DFCs was the highest-scoring ace of the RAF and Commonwealth Air Forces.

WILLIAM RHODES-MOORHOUSE

(RAF)

No 601 Sqn of the Auxiliary Air Force is famous for its 'winged' sword' badge which commemorates its position as the County of London squadron. It is also remembered for many other reasons, including the distinction of being one of the first fighter squadrons to scramble from Biggin Hill when war was declared on 3 September 1939. On that occasion its Blenheim 1fs, which had replaced its Gauntlets just after the Munich crisis, were fired on by 'friendly' AA guns on their return to base. The first action in which the unit was involved came on 28 November 1939 when six Blenheims joined forces with No 25 Sqn to attack the German seaplane base at Borkum, successfully strafing the installation and hitting several moored mine-laying seaplanes.

One of the pilots of the No 601 Sqn Blenheims was Flg Off William Henry Rhodes-Moorhouse, whose thoughts as he flew his Blenheim low over the enemy base must have gone back to 26 April 1915 when his father, 2nd/Lt William Rhodes-Moorhouse of No 2 Sqn RFC, flying a BE 2, bombed the railway junction at Courtrai from low level but was fatally wounded. He had been awarded a posthumous Victoria Cross for his gallantry. Stories of the exploits of his famous father, a national hero, prompted the young man to take an interest in aviation, and he enlisted in the Auxiliary Air Force. He qualified as a pilot and flew Demons and Gauntlets with the so-called 'weekend flyers'.

Mobilized when war was declared, Rhodes-Moorhouse anticipated that petrol rationing would soon follow, so he bought a filling station, thus ensuring that for at least some time his fellow pilots in No 601 would have no problems in obtaining fuel for their cars! In early 1940, the Blenheims gave way to Hurricanes and on 16 May Rhodes-Moorhouse found himself posted to Merville in France where 'A' Flight of No 601 was attached to No 3 Sqn. Two days later, the name Rhodes-Moorhouse was again in the news when he shot down a He 111, followed up four days later with a Bf 109. One further enemy aircraft fell to his guns in France, but his main period of success came during the three months he fought in the Battle of Britain.

On 7 July, flying with Sqn Ldr the Hon J. M. Aitken and Flg Off W. P. Clyde, contact was made with a Do 17 which the three Hurricane pilots shot into the sea north of Cherbourg, each claiming a share in its destruction.

Individual success was not far behind as, on 11 July, he and his wing man Plt Off J. W. Bland intercepted a Do 17P of 2(F)/121 and the lead Hurricane dispatched it into the sea south of the Isle of Wight. Bad weather on 16 July curtailed Luftwaffe operations, and there was only one major operation late in the afternoon, but it is this sortie around which has grown up a story about Rhodes-Moorhouse that has never been proved.

At approximately 1700 hours he was leading a formation of six Hurricanes from Tangmere when they encountered Ju 88s of 11/*KG* 54. In the combat that followed, Rhodes-Moorhouse dispatched one raider into the sea between the Needles and the mainland, and legend has it that he then flew low over the floundering bomber and threw his dinghy to the German crew. If this did happen, then he must have extracted his dinghy from its storage pack which was between his seat-type parachute and his backside, a considerable feat that would have required him to unstrap his safety and parachute harnesses in the confines of the Hurricane's cockpit whilst he was surrounded by German bombers and British fighters engaged in mortal combat. The story is even harder to believe when records show that after shooting down the first Ju 88 he chased another and may well have damaged it. It is more likely that after the combat he located the ditched bomber and radioed its position to the air-sea rescue service, but wartime propaganda saw publicity mileage in the story of a gallant pilot, the son of a Victoria Cross holder, helping his fallen foe.

The award of a DFC came in August and Rhodes-Moorhouse celebrated this with the destruction of two Bf 109s on the 11th. Sunday 18 August was a hard day for both the RAF and the Luftwaffe, one of the latter's losses being a Bf 109E-4 of 11/*JG* 2 whose pilot, Oblt R. Moellerfriedrich, baled out and was taken prisoner, the aircraft falling at Tapnall Farm, Freshwater, and the victorious pilot being the redoubtable Rhodes-Moorhouse. But time was running out for the young ace. Further shared kills on 30 August and 1 September preceded his final victory on 4 September when the Bf 110 of the *Gruppen Kommodore* of *ErpbG 20*, Hptm Boltenstern and his gunner Fw Schneider, fell to his guns over Sussex.

Two days later he became the victim of a Bf 109 when his Hurricane *P8818* was one of four No 601 Sqn aircraft to fall to the Luftwaffe in a five-minute spell just after 0930 hours. Flg Offs Davis and Rhodes-Moorhouse were killed in their burning aircraft, but the other two pilots parachuted to safety to avenge their colleagues on another day.

STANISLAW SKALSKI

(RAF)

*T*he post-war streets of Warsaw appeared to present no problems to the taxi driver as he weaved his way with undoubted skill from destination to destination. Few who rode with him were left in any doubt about his ability to handle the vehicle with deftness even in the tightest situation, which is perhaps not too surprising as the man who was now more intent on staring into a fare meter than a reflector gun sight was former RAF Wing Commander Stanislaw Skalski who, with 19½ victories, a DSO and three DFCs together with numerous other decorations, was Poland's top-scoring ace.

The contribution made to the defence of the Allied nations by many men who escaped from their native countries when the Nazis overran them can never be fully appreciated or repaid, and there are many stories outside the scope of this narrative that tell the sacrifices many of them made and continue to make. Skalski in many respects was one of the lucky ones, for after the war on his return to Poland he was imprisoned but later freed to lead a comparatively normal life and earn an honest living.

A pre-war regular officer in the Polish Air Force, the 23-year-old pilot was flying PZL P XIe fighters with No 142 (Wild Duck) Sqn when his country was invaded in September 1939. During the stubborn resistance mounted by the Poles, Skalski shot down four Dornier Do 17s and damaged another before deciding that he would be better serving the cause of freedom by escaping. With Poland on the brink of defeat, he made his way to London via the Middle East and in January 1940 enlisted in the RAF. Conversion to British methods and procedures as well as the more modern eight-gunned fighter was undertaken, and in August he joined No 501 Sqn flying Hurricanes. By early September he had doubled the score he had brought from Poland, but on the 5th whilst flying Hurricane *V6644*, he was surprised by a Bf 109 over Herne Bay and, although wounded, managed to bale out of his crashing fighter.

By June 1941, he had served with several other squadrons, then became a flight commander with No 306 Polish Sqn flying Spitfires. By the end of the summer he had added five more victories to his credit and been awarded a DFC, which he wore proudly alongside his Polish Silver Cross and Cross of Valour. A period of rest followed before he took command of another

Polish Squadron, No 317, with which he encountered and destroyed his first FW 190, receiving a Bar to his DFC in April. Perhaps his greatest honour came after he moved to Tunisia flying Spitfire IXs in what became known as 'Skalski's Circus', a unit of all the Polish pilots attached to No 145 Sqn. He became the first Pole to command a British fighter squadron, no ordinary unit but No 601 of the Desert Air Force.

On his return to England at the end of 1943, he received a second Bar to his DFC and the Polish Gold Cross, and in April 1944, now a Wing Commander, he was appointed to command No 133 (Polish No 2) Fighter Wing flying North American Mustangs in which he achieved his last two recorded kills, both FW 190s. He ended the war in select company as an instructor with 'Sailor' Malan's Advanced Gunnery School.

Returning to Poland, he was imprisoned by the Russians and during his spell of captivity must have wondered if all his efforts of the previous six years were to bring him only sadness. No doubt the many memories of his successes against a regime he hated and had fought successfully in the air carried him through this difficult period, and still floated through his mind as wayward drivers and pedestrians passed too close to his weaving taxi.

RICHARD STEVENS

(RAF)

*T*he majority of men fighting in any war have no personal reasons for
seeking revenge against the enemy; in fact, it is probably true to say that
in situations where they have come face-to-face with an enemy soldier, sailor
or airman, the comradeship of arms has been very much in evidence. But this
would not seem to be the case as far as Flt Lt Richard Stevens was concerned.
At 32, this night fighter ace was at the very upper age limit for acceptance for
pilot training when he volunteered in 1939, but his experience as a civil pilot
stood him in good stead and, as a newly commissioned pilot officer, he joined
No 151 Sqn in October 1940.

At a time when most fighter pilots were looking to end their operational
careers, Stevens was about to begin his as a Hurricane night intruder pilot.
This was at a time when airborne radar was in its infancy and the only aids to
identity in the dark skies above the British Isles were gunfire that would
lead the pilot to the scene of the activity, searchlights that might illuminate
a target, and the 'mark one eyeball' to do the rest. For this type of work, the
wide undercarriage of the Hurricane was an important asset as night
landings on fields lit by paraffin 'glim' lamps were nearly as hazardous as
searching the hostile skies where, as far as ground gunners were concerned,
there was no difference between a Hurricane, a Dornier and a Heinkel.

Stevens' pre-war flying which amounted to 400 hours at night on the
London-Paris newspaper run, gave him a distinct advantage over newer
RAF pilots embarking on night fighting, and this was no doubt a major
factor in his success. The Luftwaffe's switch to night bombing in late 1940
brought an intense campaign to get radar-equipped night fighters into
service. Interim measures involving the Defiant and Blenheim were promising, but it was not until the Beaufighter and, much later, the Mosquito
came into service that the art of night interception became fully developed.

In one of the early Luftwaffe night raids on Manchester, Stevens' wife
and children were killed, and from then on his war became a personal
vendetta against German bomber crews. In January 1941, he received
permission from his CO to fly night interception missions, his tactics being
to head for the nearest gunfire and look for enemy bombers. His first sorties
proved fruitless, but on 15 January 1941 he achieved the success he longed
for. Flying at 15,000 feet over London, he headed for tell-tale gunfire and in

the darkness suddenly caught a momentary glimpse of a Dornier Do 17.

He pulled his Hurricane into a turn and for a split second lost the hostile, then he saw it again and from that moment the German crew were doomed. The Hurricane followed the climbing bomber, always gaining on it, and at nearly 30,000 feet its slender fuselage filled the fighter's gun-sight. With all the bitterness that personal tragedy had brought building up inside him, Stevens closed even nearer then opened fire. The Dornier shook and shuddered as the force of eight Browning machine guns tore into it; pieces broke away and oil spewed back on to the Hurricane's windscreen. The bomber started to fall and Stevens followed; at 3,000 feet, the German pilot seemed to regain control but as he attempted to climb away, Stevens again fired from close range. This time, flames erupted from the dying raider and it screamed into a dive from which it never recovered. The Hurricane circled the Dornier's funeral pyre before returning to Manston.

Stevens' appetite had only been whetted, for at 0200 hours he was airborne again as more incoming raids were reported. He saw nothing until, with fuel low, he turned back towards Manston, then once more caught sight of a shadowy shape. This time it was a Heinkel 111, and its fate was identical to the Dornier, although two crew members did manage to bale out. Stevens had destroyed two enemy bombers in one night, and for this he received the DFC.

His lonely nightly vigils continued, and his tactics were always the same: get as close as possible and keep firing. Stevens claimed to have no particular dislike of individual bomber crews, but even so he pressed home his attacks, frequently pouring gunfire into the cockpit areas long after the hostile aircraft was beyond any help. On one occasion, he was so close to a Heinkel 111 when it exploded that his Hurricane was covered in debris, including blood which he refused to have removed.

After having been grounded with an ear problem for a short while, on 8 April 1941 he celebrated his return to action with two more Heinkels in one night. This was becoming a habit, and two nights later another pair fell to his guns, this time a Heinkel and a Ju 88, bringing him another DFC. By July he was the RAF's top-scoring night fighter pilot, way ahead of any with radar aids to help them. But there were many who sensed that there could only be one end.

His 14th and final victory was a Ju 88 which he shot into the sea in October. He was then posted to No 253 Sqn as a flight commander, but night bombing was becoming less frequent, so he decided to hop over the Channel and wait above enemy airfields for any bombers returning from raids. Thus he introduced night intruding which, later in the war, was to become common practice for RAF twin-engined fighters. On 12 December, he set off in a cannon-armed Hurricane to patrol the area around Gilze-Rijen in Holland, but circled the German airfield for two hours without success. Three nights later he set out again, but this time he failed to return. So died a pioneer whose total of 14 night kills in a single-engined day fighter stand as a mark of his skill and dedication, however misguided some may claim the latter to have been.

JOHN MacKAY

(RAF)

*T*iming is an essential ingredient of many aspects of warfare, not least aerial combat, and to many pilots it is second nature. They could not explain the how and why of it any more than, for example, the sportsmen of today can explain how their timing enables them to be in the right place at the right time to execute the perfect cover-drive or score the perfect goal. It is not only in gunnery that timing is an important asset, but also every aspect of flying including aerobatics, and there are many stories of pilots who excelled at this art, causing their opponents to crash by forcing them into manoeuvres from which there was no hope of recovery. One such ace was a Canadian, Sqn Ldr John MacKay, one of the few pilots to have recorded jet victories in the Second World War and Korea.

Born in Cloverdale, British Columbia, John MacKay joined the RCAF in 1942 and was posted to No 401 Sqn with the 2nd Tactical Air Force in August 1944, thus coming late to the ETO. However, he soon made up for lost time when he damaged a Bf 109 on 25 September. On 5 October, with four other pilots, he shared in the destruction of a Me 262, the first jet fighter to fall in combat with the British Commonwealth air forces.

On Christmas Day he recorded his first individual victory, a Bf 109, and on New Year's Day followed this with a FW 190, a share in another Me 262, then the first of his victories in which he used no ammunition. Seeing another FW 190, he set off after the German fighter which, in trying to avoid the attentions of the Canadian, flew into the ground. He then engaged a Bf 109 which, in trying to match the superb aerobatics of the Spitfire pilot, also misjudged a turn and flew straight into *terra firma*. So, on one day MacKay accounted for 1½ German fighters with gunfire and two with aerobatic skills.

Two weeks later, MacKay encountered a flight of FW 190s, used his guns on two and then took the third on an aerial ballet in which he called the steps and eventually brought the German to earth, once again without firing a shot. On 28 March, now a flight commander with a DFC to his credit, he found six patrolling Bf 109s; although alone and with a long-range belly tank on his Spitfire, he had no hesitation in engaging the enemy, and even with the handicap of the tank found little difficulty in giving another superb aerobatic display during which he used his guns to account for two of the

109s. He also proved his all-round ability when, on 16 April, he strafed a German airfield, damaging three Arado Ar 234 jet bombers. Four days later, he closed his Second World War account with another Bf 109. His total stood at 11.2, and in May he was awarded a Bar to his DFC.

Staying in the RCAF after the war, he became CO of No 416 Sqn, then, during the Korean War, he went on an exchange posting to the 51st Fighter Group. On 30 June 1953, whilst flying an F-86, he shot down a MiG 15, thus becoming one of the very few Commonwealth pilots to have scored victories over jet aircraft from two different generations.

RICHARD BONG

(USAAC)

*I*n his diary detailing his experiences in the Far East, Sqn Ldr 'Bunny' Stone, CO of No 17 Sqn (see under Frank Carey), records how in Cairo he and his pilots had been told that the Japanese were short-sighted, poor shots and had inferior aeroplanes. He subsequently found to his cost that these comments were wrong on all three counts. True, the Japanese aircraft lacked some of the sophistication of their western counterparts, not having armour plating and being made of extremely light alloy with some control surfaces from balsa skinned with aluminium, but they were highly manoeuvrable, had a good rate of climb and could turn very tightly. In the main, Japanese pilots were far from being poor shots, had extremely good eyesight, and their culture, which enabled them to look at life and fighting for the Emperor in a rather different way from both the Allies and the Germans, combined to make them formidable opponents. It is therefore aggravating when less knowledgeable commentators tend to dismiss the achievements of Western aces fighting in the Far East, in the same way that they sometimes discount the claims of Luftwaffe pilots on the Russian Front. One man who has suffered in this way is America's leading Second World War ace, Major Richard Bong, who scored all his 40 victories in the Pacific theatre flying the P-38 Lightning.

It is fascinating to find that the characteristics and careers of many aces are very similar, and it is often possible to trace what appears to be a common link, but which, on the other hand, might be total coincidence. In the case of Richard Bong, his mother was Scottish and his father Swedish, similar to the parentage of George Beurling, and, like the Canadian, Bong had the same determination to fly and be successful. He joined the US Air Corps in 1941 and, after getting his 'wings', became an instructor.

This was far from his liking, for he had joined the Air Force to fly fighters, but eventually his persistent badgering paid off and he was posted to Australia with the 49th FG of the 5th Air Force, arriving in September 1942 with the first P-38s, aircraft that were to make an immediate and lasting impact on the Japanese. Three months after his arrival, and following a working-up period, Bong was in action getting his first two kills, a 'Val' dive-bomber and a Zero on 27 December 1942.

The immensely powerful P-38 was deadly in the hands of an expert, and there was no doubting that Bong easily fell into this category. By March 1943, his score had risen to nine, six of which were Army Ki 43 'Oscar' fighters. He then encountered a lean patch until the end of July when, on the 26th, he shot down two more 'Oscars' and two Kawasaki Ki 61 'Tonys', which, with two earlier victories in the month together with another Tony on the 28th, took his total to 16, which equalled the previous highest score by a 5th Air Force pilot. He was out of action until October, then made up for the delay with five victories in November, after which he was sent back to the USA for some well-earned leave.

On his return to action in February 1944, he found that Thomas McGuire of the 475th was level with him, and, although Bong was now officially attached to 5th AF Headquarters, he was allowed to fly in combat situations with any unit he chose. This roving commission suited the ace, and he wasted no time in taking full advantage of it by seeking out the Japanese whenever he could. By April he had become the first Air Corps pilot to pass Rickenbacker's First World War total, and, with 27 kills to his credit, was the top-scoring American pilot at that time. Soon after he returned to the States for a lecture tour, he learned that one of his probables had been confirmed so his total was increased to 28 which kept him level with Bob Johnson who had briefly passed him.

Officialdom sometimes seems to move in strange ways, and it was with some surprise that Bong was sent on a gunnery course to improve his shooting; however, the main reason was more likely to equip him for instructional duties, because in September 1944 he returned to New Guinea as a gunnery instructor. He was soon back in the unofficial neck-and-neck race with McGuire, both men adding to their scores in September, Bong getting five and McGuire three. The latter pilot had scored five during Bong's absence, so the gap had been narrowed by only two. In November, both scored three times, then on 7 December each bagged another pair; on the 15th and 17th of the month, Bong accounted for a couple of 'Oscars' to take his total to 40, against his rival's 31.

In November, General Douglas MacArthur presented Bong with the Congressional Medal of Honour and then in December ordered him home. It seemed as though the field was clear for McGuire to surge ahead, especially as on Christmas Day he took his total to 34 with three Zeros, and accounted for four more on Boxing Day. With 38 kills he was now just two short of Bong's final tally, then fate took a hand. On 7 January 1945, McGuire's section was bounced by two experienced Japanese pilots; turning to the aid of his two inexperienced wing men, McGuire pulled his P-38 too tight and with the extra drag of wing tanks it spun in and he was killed.

In America, meanwhile, Richard Bong was facing a new challenge, that of the jet age. He became a service test pilot working up the Lockheed P-80 Shooting Star which it was hoped to introduce into combat before the end of the war. This was not to be, but on 6 August 1945 the aircraft claimed America's top ace when Bong was killed during take-off when the P-80 suffered a flame-out and crashed.

FRANCIS GABRESKI

(USAAC)

*T*he F-80 Shooting Star was a contemporary of the British Gloster Meteor and the German Messerschmitt Me 262, but, unlike the other two, it just failed to see operational service during the Second World War. However, neither the British nor the German jet met the other in combat, which left the field for this debut wide open to the American fighter, since it was one of the front-line jets equipping the American Air Force in the Far East when the Korean War started in the summer of 1950. On 8 November 1950, a flight of four F-80s was flying top cover to B-29 bombers attacking Sinuija airfield when six of the new Russian-built swept-wing MiG 15 fighters were scrambled from their base at Antung, quickly climbed to 30,000 feet, divided into pairs and dived on the American fighters. The first ever air-to-air combat between jet fighters was about to start.

Among the young American pilots was 1st Lt Russell Brown, who tenaciously clung to the tail of a diving MiG and, although only one of his .5 calibre nose-mounted machine-guns was working, he eventually detected strikes on the MiG before it suddenly blew apart. Brown was one of the new generation of jet fighter pilots who were to carve their names in aviation history in skies far from their native America. Their skills flying the straight-winged F-80 enabled them to survive against the aerodynamically superior Russian fighter until the arrival of the F-86 Sabre which tended to level the differences.

By contrast, among these young pilots there was a core of older men who had experienced combat in the hostile skies over Europe, and whose experience in dogfighting was to prove invaluable even though the pace and altitude had increased beyond their wildest dreams since the heady days of 1944-45 when most of them cut their teeth. Among the 39 USAF pilots to become Sabre aces in Korea were 13 who between them had scored 100 victories in the Second World War, and the leading ace of this select band was Col Francis Gabreski. With 31 kills, he was America's top-scoring European ace, and had it not been for a spot of high ground near Koblenz he may well never have reached the Korean skies.

On 20 July 1944, Gabreski who, like his friend Bob Johnson, scored all his victories flying P-47s, was due to fly his last combat mission in Europe before a rest. It was indeed followed by a long rest, but not of the type Gabreski or his seniors had envisaged. With 28 air and three ground victories (counted by the 8th Air Force) to his credit, Gabreski was just ahead of Johnson in total kills. On that fateful day he was strafing a German airfield when, during a low pass, his propeller hit rising ground and he was forced to crash-land. He avoided capture for five days, but was then caught and spent the rest of the war in Stalag Luft 1 near Barth.

Gabreski was born on 28 January 1919 to Polish immigrants, and joined the Army Air Corps in 1940 after two years in medical school. He initially served with the 45th Fighter Squadron at Wheeler Field, Hawaii, and was there when Pearl Harbor was attacked. In 1942 he was assigned to the 56th Fighter Group, but on arrival in England was seconded to No 315 (Polish) Sqn RAF at Northolt, where his fluent Polish helped ease initial language problems. He flew 13 operational trips on Spitfire Vs without success before returning to the 56th, when his career started to follow a similar pattern to that of Johnson, although unlike him he did not have the lone hunting streak that required disciplining. Like many crack pilots, however, he did have his own quirks; for example, he strongly believed that with his ammunition tanks full, his P-47's wings were too heavy to enable him to turn inside a Bf 109 or FW 190, so he only flew with them half full, and this load never included tracer shells as he felt that these warned opponents that they were under fire.

His theories seemed to work for him as his first victory was a FW 190 downed on 24 August 1943 when he was a flight commander with the 56th Fighter Group. Two Bf 110s on 26 November brought him ace status. By the end of the year he had scored eight, two less than Johnson, but he continued to score steadily until, by 8 May 1944, when he was commanding the 61st Fighter Squadron, his tally stood at 19. A hat-trick of victories over FW 190s on 22 May, five more in June and another on 5 July levelled his total with that of Johnson in air-to-air combat situations.

On his return from captivity, he flew as a test pilot before leaving the peace-time air force for a short while. He re-enlisted in 1946 and flew with the 4th Fighter-Interceptor Wing which he commanded in Korea between July 1951 and April 1952. During this time he showed that he had lost none of his aerial skills and proved time and again that the original fighter pilot's dictum of getting close before firing paid dividends. Flying his F-86 Sabre with the same verve he had handled the P-47, he added 6½ MiG 15s to his original score of 31 before returning to the USA.

In 1956, Gabreski took over command of the 354th Fighter Group flying the first truly supersonic fighter to see squadron service, the North American F100 Super Sabre. 'Gabby', as he was known in air force circles, retired in 1967 with the rank of Colonel.

ROBERT S. JOHNSON

(USAAC)

*T*alk of RAF and Commonwealth aces, and the subconscious mind always seems to link them with those outstanding British fighter aircraft of the Second World War, the Spitfire, Hurricane and Mosquito. Similarly, when thoughts turn to the men of the US Air Forces, the P-47 Thunderbolt, P-51 Mustang and P-38 Lightning are to the fore. It is also true that some pilots will always be associated with a particular aircraft and one such man is Robert S. Johnson of the 56th Fighter Group USAAC, whose name is synonymous with the enormous P-47 Thunderbolt, known to its crews as the 'Jug', in which he shot down 28 German aircraft, all but four being single-engined fighters.

In the summer of 1928, eight-year-old Robert Johnson would have much preferred to have been fishing than bouncing along a dusty country road near Lawton, Oklahoma, in his father's 1926 Essex. But it was a family trip to an air show at nearby Post Field, and the young Johnson, together with his two older sisters and the family dog, were being taken on a picnic to share one of dad's interests, so, for that day at least, fishing had to take a back seat. However, the outing turned out to be significant, for by the end of the afternoon young Robert had decided that he was going to be an Army fighter pilot.

This decision did not completely replace his original thoughts of becoming a cowboy, fireman or engine driver, for when he was old enough he took a variety of jobs which enabled him to take private flying lessons. A loan from the Dean of Cameron Junior College, Dr Clarence Breedlove, enabled him to obtain his licence, then, in 1941, he left his engineering studies and joined the Air Corps as a Cadet. Although an accomplished pilot, Johnson was less than outstanding at some subjects, including gunnery, and it began to look as though his ambition to fly fighters would be still-born. Indeed towards the end of his advanced flying training, instructors pointed out that the future was in commercial flying and in the post-war world it would be ex-*bomber* pilots who would be flying the new air routes around the world.

In February 1942 Johnson got married and promised his new bride that he would volunteer for bombers, so this and the advice of his instructors nearly saw the embryo fighter pilot follow an entirely different road.

However, on 3 July 1942 he received his coveted silver wings and with them instructions to report to a fighter conversion school. Robert Johnson was about to make an indelible mark in the European Theatre of Operations (ETO).

Johnson arrived inEngland with 'Hub' Zemke's 56th Fighter Group on 13 January 1943 and flew his first operational sortie in April in Zemke's number four slot escorting B-17s. Although the fighters encountered FW 190s, Johnson only claimed hits on one of the German fighters. Like many other aces, he disagreed with the defined tactics of his senior officers and had his own pet theories. At this time it was the policy of the American escort fighters to wait until the enemy engaged them; Johnson always felt that this was wrong, and that if enemy fighters were seen they should be engaged.

On 13 June 1943, flying over Northern France, he put his theory to the test. Spotting 12 FW 190s several thousand feet below his formation of P-47s, Johnson broke away and screamed after the Germans. He arrived among them at some considerable speed and his six blazing .5 calibre machine-guns cut one of the FW 190s to pieces before the enemy fighters could react. Climbing hard to rejoin Col Zemke and the rest of his section, Johnson soon found the German pilots were on his tail, and there followed a swirling dogfight in which two more FW 190s fell to Col Zemke's guns. On their return to base, the Colonel made it quite clear to the elated Johnson that if he broke formation again he would be grounded. The young American fought all such temptation and by the end of the year his score stood at 10.

He had survived a close call when, obeying orders, he was bounced together with the rest of his formation by a group of Bf 109s, then, much to his relief, the 8th Air Force relaxed its policies and adopted more aggressive tactics which allowed fighter pilots to break formation, albeit after advising the leader, and engage enemy fighters. The idea was that if a section of, say, four aircraft saw enemy fighters, two would go after them while the other two would act as top cover. This seemed to work well for Johnson for, throughout his two tours of operations, he never lost one of his wing men.

By the spring of 1944, he was well established among America's top flyers and commanded the 61st Fighter Squadron. The mammoth air battles over Europe, as German fighter pilots fought valiantly to defend their homeland against the American daylight bomber offensive, saw the P-47s venture right to Berlin with their charges, although they were limited in their defensive tactics by the long-range belly tanks that enabled them to make so long a journey.

On 15 March 1944, nine days after the P-47s had first visited Berlin, Johnson accounted for three FW 190s and a Bf 110 to take his total to 22, thus passing the record of Walker Mahurin to become the top Eighth ace at that time. Four more kills in April took his tally to that of the First World War ace Eddie Rickenbacker, and the name of Major Johnson became a household word back in the USA, alongside that of his Pacific theatre rival, Richard Bong. Both men returned to the States to give lecture tours and promote war bonds, but Bong returned to operations and took his final score to 40. Two of Johnson's 'damaged' claims were subsequently confirmed as kills which raised his final score to 28, making him level with Francis Gabreski as the top-scoring American aces of the ETO, although if one ground victory is added to Gabreski's total, he just surpasses Johnson, the Thunderbolt ace.

DAVID McCAMPBELL

(USAAC)

*T*he average age of aircrew in the Second World War was 25, and most fighter pilots were slightly younger; indeed, any one older than that was considered to be 'getting on' and those few who were beyond 30 were looked upon by their young companions as being positively elderly. There are, of course, exceptions to every rule, and it is not therefore too surprising to find that some aces were not the young dashing pilots that many people associate with that accolade, and into this category falls the United States Navy's number one ace, Commander David S. McCampbell of VF-15.

Campbell was born in Bessemer, Alabama, and in 1934, at the age of 24, he joined the US Navy. He was thus already a very experienced pilot when his country entered the war in 1941, and this kept him firmly entrenched in the States until mid-1943, when, at the age of 33, he took over the command of the Air Group aboard the carrier USS *Essex*, flying F6F Hellcats, and headed for the Far East. His former squadron, VF-15, formed part of the carrier's Air Group and it was with this unit that McCampbell chose to fly.

He had to wait until 11 June 1944 to record his first kill, a Mitsubishi A6M Zeke (Zero), which fell to his guns near Saipan in the Marianas. Just over a week later, on 19 June, he was very much involved in what has become known as the Great Marianas 'Turkey Shoot', when US Navy pilots accounted for 300 Japanese aircraft for the loss of only 16 Hellcats. On that occasion, McCampbell flew a morning and afternoon sortie, shooting down five Yokosuka D4Y (Judy) dive-bombers before lunch, and followed the main course with two Zeros in the afternoon.

During September he enjoyed another multiple victory with seven in two days, but his greatest achievement came on 24 October when US forces landed on Leyte and the *Essex* was in the Task Force covering the assault. McCampbell, who now had 21 kills to his name, had been instructed not to fly on air defence sorties although he was permitted to lead the air group in strike operations. On this day, however, the Japanese mounted a big counter-attack against the landings and the carrier's fighters were held back to defend the Task Force; McCampbell was on board when a large force of hostile aircraft was detected heading towards the Navy ships.

The Hellcats were immediately launched and every pilot was required, so McCampbell needed no further excuse to join the mission. He was flying top cover with Lt Roy Rushing as his wing man, and, after dispatching his main force to make contact with the Japanese, he and Rushing circled and waited for any aircraft that might attempt a high-level approach. Before long, over 40 Zeros and 'Oscars' appeared, each carrying bombs beneath its wings. The two Hellcat pilots dived on them, but the Japanese formed a defensive circle which was difficult to penetrate. However, as the Navy pilots were only some 30 miles from their carrier, and the Japanese were a long way from their Manila bases, time was very much in favour of the two Americans.

With fuel dwindling rapidly, the Japanese had to make their move, and this came when two broke the circle and dived towards the sea. By this time, McCampbell's calls on the R/T for support had been answered by the arrival of another F6F, and the trio of American fighters took the chance presented to them and once more dived into the Japanese formation. For the next 90 minutes, the Americans harassed the Japanese fighter-bombers, some of which jettisoned their bomb loads and were thus able to meet the Hellcats on more equal terms. The F6F which had joined McCampbell and Rushing had been in action earlier, so was lower on fuel and ammunition than the other two; therefore, after downing at least four enemy aircraft it returned to the *Essex*, leaving the pair to continue the fight.

The tactics adopted by the Navy flyers were to keep above the enemy fighters and swoop every time one tried to either get away or climb to intercept them. They had the total advantage, apart from in numbers, and as the enemy pilots became more and more aware of their hopeless situation, especially as their fuel was by now getting very close to danger level, they tried to break off the combat and head home. However, on each occasion the Hellcats swooped, one covering the other's tail, and on nearly every dive an enemy fighter fell. By the time the running fight ended, more than 20 Japanese fighters had been shot down or seriously damaged. McCampbell claimed seven Zeros, two 'Oscars' and two more probables, and Rushing five Zeros, an 'Oscar' and three probables. The two pilots estimated that they had made between 15 and 20 passes at the enemy formation, and when they landed their Hellcats were virtually flying on the fumes from their fuel tanks, and McCampbell had just two rounds of ammunition left.

McCampbell's nine victories were a record for an American pilot in one sortie. The fighting in the skies above Leyte continued, and McCampbell scored three more victories to take his final total to 34, which coincidentally was also his age at that time. The action of 24 October brought him the award of a Congressional Medal of Honour to add to his Navy Cross, Silver Star, Legion of Merit, Distinguished Flying Cross with Gold Stars, and Air Medal. His score was also the highest by a US Navy pilot, and only six short of America's top ace, Richard Bong, proving that even an 'old man' could emulate the youngsters.

WALKER H. MAHURIN

(USAAC)

Col Walker Mahurin returned from the Korean War confident that a sound career awaited him in the USAF, but sadly he was soon disillusioned, for after he had been shot down in his Sabre on 13 May 1952 during an experimental fighter-bomber sortie, he had been subjected to the then new technique of interrogation known as 'brainwashing'. Using this technique, the Communists had eventually persuaded the Second World War ace, who had accounted for 3½ MiG 15s, to sign a document admitting that he had dropped chemical bombs on North Korean targets. 'Bud' Mahurin only signed when he was convinced that the paper contained so many errors and contradictory statements that it would not stand close analysis, but in that assumption he was entirely wrong, for the American authorities did not understand the techniques that had been used, and Mahurin was court-martialled. Later, the findings of the court were squashed and he was exonerated, but by then the damage had been done, and Mahurin had left the service he had loved and served loyally for 14 years and entered civil aviation whose gain was certainly the American nation's loss.

'Bud' had been given a pleasure flight in a Stinson in 1925 when he was just seven years old, and from then on his sole aim in life had been to become a pilot. His family were not from one of the wealthier echelons of the Fort Wayne, Indiana, society, and the young Mahurin had an uphill struggle to finance himself through part-time study to graduation, after which he became an apprentice engineer. He joined the government's civilian pilot training scheme and learned to fly in his spare time; enlisting into the Air Corps in 1940, he was assigned to the 56th Fighter Group flying Thunderbolts, arriving in England in January 1943.

By May, he was a flight leader with the rank of Captain, and in July his career may well have come to a premature end when, in formation with a B24, he flew too close to the bomber, whose propellers severed the tail from his P-47. Mahurin managed to bale out of the spinning fighter and landed, a shaken but wiser man. His confidence was, however, soon restored by his first combat success which he achieved on 17 August when he shot down a pair of FW 190s. Flying just south of Beauvais on 9 September, he bagged another FW 190 then, on 4 October, scored three in a day with a trio of Bf

110s near Dueren. He achieved a notable landmark on 26 November when three more Bf110s gave him the honour of being the first 8th Air Force pilot to reach double figures.

His score continued to mount with a variety of types falling to his guns including a pair of Ju 88s and five Bf 109s. On 27 March 1944 he became the first American pilot to reach 20 victories, but on this occasion the rear gunner of the Dornier Do 17 he shared with three others brought his tour to a premature end. Accurate fire from the German damaged his P-47, forcing him to bale out for the second time in his career. This time he fell into enemy-occupied territory, but evaded capture and with the help of the French Resistance managed to get back to England on 7 May 1944.

He then returned to the USA to lecture about his experiences, but managed to return to operational flying on P-51s with the 3rd Air Commando Group in New Guinea, the Philippines and Okinawa, where once again mixed fortunes awaited him. On 14 January 1945, he added a Japanese bomber to his original 20, but a few days later was forced to crash into the sea off Formosa, but was soon rescued. He stayed in the Air Force after the war and managed to obtain a short detachment to Korea with the 51st FIW at the end of 1951. On 6 January 1952, he scored his first MiG 15 kill and added another two together with a shared before the fateful 13 May.

Bud Mahurin was a superb fighter pilot who proved his worth and patriotism in two conflicts during which he was awarded the DSC, Silver Star, DFC and Air Medal.

ROBIN OLDS

(USAAC)

*T*here is a story that when the first F-4 Phantom II arrived in England, a Royal Navy Fleet Air Arm pilot stared at the unusual configuration of the aircraft and asked with some incredulity, 'Has it been put together the right way up?'. There are similar stories about the first Lockheed P-38 Lightnings that arrived in Europe during the Second World War, as this huge (for the period) twin-boomed fighter was just as remarkable to the pilots of those days as was the Phantom to a later generation.

A pilot who held the rare distinction of flying the F-4 and the P-38 in combat, and scoring kills with both aircraft, was Col Robin Olds who, when he embarked on the path to becoming an ace in 1944, never thought that 20 years later he would be flying and fighting at twice the altitude and three times the speed with a weapons system that in 1944 could have stepped straight from the pages of science fiction.

Olds was born in July 1922 in California to an Air Force family, so it was natural that he should follow in his father's footsteps, father being Major-General Robert Olds, who commanded the first B-17 Group to be formed in the 'thirties. Olds junior arrived in England in 1944 with the last fighter group to join the 8th, the 479th, known after their CO, Lt Col Kyle Riddle, as 'Riddles Raiders'. The unit was based at Wattisham and equipped with P-38Js, which it first took into action on 26 May 1944.

Lt Robin Olds made his first kill on 14 August 1944 with a double victory whilst serving with the 434th FS, and followed this with three more successes on 25 August to reach ace status in just two combat engagements. By February 1945, with nine victories to his credit, he was the 8th Air Force's top-scoring ace with the P-38, and, on conversion to the P-51, showed that he was just at home in the single-seater, scoring another double on 19 March and concluding his aerial victories on 7 April with his twelfth victory. To these he was able to add 11 strafing successes, making his final score for the Second World War 23. All his aircraft were named 'Scat', and among his aerial victories was an Aradao Ar 234 jet bomber. It is of interest to note that the 479th was the first American Fighter Group in Europe to meet German jets in combat, when Capt Arthur Jeffrey claimed a probable after engaging a Me 163 on 29 July 1944 (which, to be strictly accurate, was powered by a rocket motor and not a jet engine, but the principal of propulsion was, of course, the same).

Major Olds, not surprisingly, stayed in the Air Force after the war and in 1946 came second in the Thompson Jet Trophy Race during the National Air Races. He served the peace-time Air Force well and returned to England to command the 81st TFW at Bentwaters. In 1966 he was assigned to the 8th TFW in South-east Asia flying the F-4C.

In the days of the Second World War, fighter pilots in their 'thirties had been the exception rather than the rule, the average age being close to 21. Few of those young men, and indeed the public who were brought up on the fighter pilot image of a clear-eyed square-jawed young flyer, would have believed that men twice their age would have been capable of flying, let alone fighting in, jet fighter aircraft in combat. But that is exactly what Robin Olds and several other Second World War veterans did in Vietnam, and, moreover, made a considerable success of it.

During 1967, the USAF claimed the destruction of 77 MiG 17 and 21 fighters in air-to-air combat over North Vietnam, the majority falling to the guns and missiles of F-4 Phantoms which at that time were usually assigned top-cover to F105 Thunderchiefs that were carrying out low-level bombing and ground attack roles. One of the largest and most successful actions occurred on 6 January 1967 when the 8th TFW claimed seven MiG 21s without loss over the Red River Valley area. One of the Russian jets fell to Col Olds and his RIO (Radar Intercept Officer), Lt Steve Croker.

The RIO, who was often known as the 'GIB' (Guy In the Backseat), played a vital role in interception work, and later in that conflict Capt Charles DeBellevue, who flew in the back of Capt Steven Ritchie's F-4, was acclaimed as the highest-scoring jet ace in Vietnam with six victories. Four of these were scored with Ritchie and two with another pilot. Olds and Croker scored another victory on 4 May and 16 days later added two more to become the top-scoring American fighter crew, a record that stood until 1972 when Lt Randy Cunningham and William Driscoll of the USN flying from the USS *Constellation* took their score to five to become Phantom aces, an honour they shared with Capt Steve Ritchie (pilot) and Capt Charles DeBellevue (RIO) of the USAF. Cunningham and Driscoll shot down three MiG 17s on 10 May 1972, the last of which was piloted by the leading Communist pilot Col Nguyon Toon who had 13 US aircraft to his credit. In fact, the Phantom that brought about his downfall was so badly damaged in the combat that Cunningham and Driscoll had to eject into the sea.

During the Vietnam conflict, USAF fighters accounted for 135 victories, the most successful being the 8th TFW with 38.5, which in 1967 had been Col Old's command. The sophisticated weapons, the electronic aids and countermeasures, and the speed of aerial combat, not to mention other factors such as height, size of aircraft and so on, all contributed to a considerable change from the days of the first jet combats in Korea, and were a far cry from the days of the Second World War when the *total* of USAF kills (135) was not an unusual score for a single Luftwaffe ace; moreover, the 8ths 38.5 was achieved by several Allied aces, but amongst them Robin Olds proved that even 'old men' could still mix it with the best of a younger generation.

DAVID SCHILLING

(USAAC)

*I*n the mid-1950s, the USAF, which it had become on separation from the Army in 1948, was becoming more and more re-established in England as the world political situation developed into a 'Cold War' between East and West. Many of the men now in command positions were veterans of the Second World War and had seen service in England, especially East Anglia, where their accents were still very familiar in contrast to the blue uniforms that had replaced the drab khaki of the days when they were at the controls of B-17s, B-24s, P-51s and P-47s. Their friendliness and outgoing personalities were also still very much the same, and the fewer restrictions of peace-time England gave them a much wider scope for some of their indulgences, as of course did the – at that time – all-powerful dollar.

One of the most coveted possessions of many of the young officers and NCOs was a British sports car, and it was not unusual to see TR2s, Austin-Healey 100s, Jaguar XK120s, all with left-hand drives, parked near flight lines and outside the nearby country pubs. On 14 August 1956, near Eriswell in Suffolk, one of the more exotic examples of the very powerful specialist cars, in this case an Allard, struck a concrete bridge post and the 38-year-old American driving it was killed.

It was a sad though not too unusual event, but this traffic accident took the life of a man who had survived 360 operational flying hours in 132 combat sorties during which he had scored a total of 22.5 air and 10.5 strafing victories. He was Colonel David Schilling, serving in the peace-time USAF as a staff officer, and his combined total of air and ground victories placed him second to Col John Meyer (combined total 37) in the list of USAAC European aces, and in sixth place if only aerial kills are counted.

Schilling had been amongst the first wave of American pilots to arrive in England (apart from those already mentioned who served with the Eagle Squadrons). He was from Kansas and had graduated with a geology degree in June 1939 before volunteering for service with the USAAC later the same year. On qualifying as a fighter pilot, he was posted to the 8th Pursuit Group at Langley, and moved with them to New York before joining the 56th Fighter Group on its formation. He was one of the 8th's first aces and eventually took over command of the Group from its most famous leader, 'Hub' Zemke.

Schilling was a natural leader and a born fighter pilot; his gunnery was quite remarkable and his total of 22.5 air kills were accounted for in just over 12 months, a period which was of course broken up by periods of leave and ground attachments. He opened his account with two victories on 2 October 1943 when a Bf 109 and FW 190 fell to the guns of his P-47 over Emden. Eight days later he had scored the mandatory five to give him the coveted ace status, and by the end of the year his score stood at seven.

He commanded No 62 FS but in August 1943 was promoted to Major and became the Executive Officer for the 56th FG. Three months later he was a Lieutenant Colonel and, at the turn of the year, acted as deputy CO which gave him valuable experience for when he took over the Group the following August. During this time he flew many escort missions and on 8 March 1944 was one of the first pilots to claim victory over the new Messerschmitt 410 that was beginning to be seen in increasing numbers. His score mounted steadily with 'doubles' being achieved on two occasions, a hat-trick on 21 September over Holland with three FW 190s, and then perhaps his greatest achievement two days before Christmas with five in one day.

This 'nap hand' came his way over Bonn when the Luftwaffe mounted a major counter-attack against B-17s and B-24s attacking marshalling yards, communication centres and railway junctions. In poor weather conditions, the 56th flew a Fighter Sweep in their P-47s whilst P-51s acted as escorts. Among the confirmed victories claimed by the 56th were three Bf 109s and two FW 190s to Col Schilling.

In January 1945 he became 'Exec' to the 65 FW, and then Director of Intelligence to the 8th Air Force before returning to the USA on the cessation of hostilities in May 1945. His acquaintance with the 56th was renewed after the war and he led the unit to England in July 1948 when it had the honour of flying its P-80 Shooting Stars on the first transatlantic jet flight by the newly created USAF.

With a DSC with one Oak Leaf Cluster, a Silver Star with two Oak Leaf Clusters, a DFC with eight Oak Leaf Clusters, an Air Medal, the British DFC, and a *Croix de Guerre* to his credit, this highly decorated and talented officer was clearly destined for the very top echelons of the USAF, until that fateful summer day when his sports car left a British country road.

HEINZ BÄR

(LUFTWAFFE)

The controversy that sometimes still rages about the claims of Luftwaffe pilots is often centred on the argument that many of the highest-scoring aces recorded all their kills on the Eastern Front. To a certain extent this is true, but it does not mean that Russian pilots were in the main inferior to any others; what is quite often conveniently overlooked is that the front lines were so close and, in general, the German fighters so superior, that pilots could fly many sorties every day and on each one they were almost sure to be engaged in aerial combat. However, for every argument there is always a strong counter and in the case of high-scoring Luftwaffe aces, Heinz Bär is one of the many who adds strength to the argument against the 'Russian Front' theory. For Bär, who like Galland fought throughout the whole of the Second World War, scored prolifically on the Eastern *and* Western Fronts as well as in the Mediterranean and North Africa. Starting the war as an NCO flying Bf 109s, he ended with a total of 220 kills and has the distinction of being the highest-scoring jet ace with 16 Allied aircraft falling to the guns of his Me 262.

Born in Leipzig in March 1913, Heinz Bär always wanted to be an airline pilot and took the first step towards this ambition by gaining his private pilot's licence through one of the many sports flying clubs that flourished in the Germany of the 1930s. He enlisted in the Luftwaffe in 1937, and was an Unteroffizier when the Second World War started.

His first confirmed kill came on 25 September 1939 when he downed a French Air Force Curtiss P-36. During the battles of France and Britain he flew with Moelder's *JG* 51 and became the Luftwaffe's top-scoring NCO pilot with 17 victories. Like many of those who achieved ace status, it was at some cost to the Luftwaffe, and he survived several close shaves with the RAF culminating in his baling out over the Channel on 2 September after combat with Spitfires of No 603 Sqn.

He was commissioned at the end of 1940 and, on 22 June, formed part of the force tasked with gaining air superiority during the Russian invasion. His skill and gunnery saw his score mount rapidly and by August he had reached 60 and received the coveted Ritterkreuz with Oak Leaves. On 30 August he scored six kills in one day, but the following day was forced to bale out.

This time there was no German rescue service to recover him. Landing in hostile country, he managed to avoid detection and walked back to the German lines suffering from injuries which kept him grounded until early in 1942. A further 24 victories on the Eastern Front took his total to 90 before he took command of *JG* 77 and swopped the snows of the East for the sun of the Mediterranean, where he operated initially from Sicily.

During the Malta campaign he scored four victories and, later in the year, operating over North Africa, he accounted for another 22. In the air battles over Tunisia and Tripoli his tenacity brought him a further 39, taking his Middle East total to 65 and making him the third highest scoring ace in that theatre.

Following the retreat from North Africa in 1943 he found himself with 11/*JG* 1 flying FW 190s in defence of the Reich. It was during this period that he perfected the head-on attack against the massed formations of USAAC B-17s and B-24s, accounting for at least 24 of the American bombers to take his total to 202 by April 1944.

He had now been in almost continuous action since 1939 and his health began to suffer; nonetheless, after only a short rest he was appointed to command *JG* 3, and led them in the ill-fated Operation Bodenplatte on 1 January 1945, during which he shot down two British fighters to take his total to 204. With the Luftwaffe in its death throes, he was one of the pilots to prove that there was still a considerable sting in its tail. Flying Me 262s as commander of 111/*EJG* 2, he accounted for 16 Allied aircraft during March and April 1945 to end the war with a total of 220 kills achieved in 1,000 combat sorties. This tally put him in eighth place overall in the listing of top German aces, and second to Marseille in the destruction of British and American aircraft. Affectionately known as 'Pritzel', this colourful and popular pilot, the first jet ace, was killed in April 1957 in a light aircraft crash.

WALTHER DAHL

(LUFTWAFFE)

The massacre of RAF Wellington bombers in daylight raids during December 1939 brought home the lesson that mutual protection by massed armament in bomber formations did not work, and led the RAF to adopt a policy of night bombing using the bomber stream technique. The USAAC, however, stuck with the original philosophy, and their heavily armed B-17 and B-24 bombers flying in box formations were much more able to offer a stronger defence against fighters than the Wellingtons. Until the introduction of long-range escorts, the bombers continued to suffer at the hands of defending fighters, but in turn took a heavy toll of Luftwaffe day fighters.

To attack a massed formation from the rear was a tricky operation and the usual technique was to gain height advantage and make a diving pass through the bomber formation. However, aces like Egon Mayer and Heinz Bär developed a technique of frontal attack, where the closing speed was very much greater, giving their cannon-armed fighters a distinct advantage. The frontal armament of the bombers was more limited than the combined rear defensive weaponry, and the gunners were faced with targets which, although increasing in size by the second, were travelling very fast, thus reducing the time they were within range. Increased forward armament like the chin turret of the B-17G helped, but there can be little doubt that a heavily armed aircraft such as the FW 190 flown by even moderate *experten* were a frightening sight to bomber crews as they tore head-on towards them, apparently immune to defending fire.

To break formation was suicidal, and to try to turn away could lead to collisions. It is not too surprising, therefore, that many Luftwaffe pilots became so-called four-engined bomber aces from their successful use of the head-on attack, although it must be appreciated that not every kill was achieved by this method. Top ace in this category was Herbert Rollwage of *JG* 53, with 44 bombers in his total of 102 kills, but close on his heels with 36 such kills from a total of 128 was a man who fought throughout the war in the Mediterranean, on the Eastern Front and in defence of the Reich, and became Inspector General of Dayfighters: Oberst Walther Dahl.

Like many pilots, Dahl had his own particular trademark and a liking for a particular aircraft, in his case the FW 190A-8/R-8. This was a heavily

Above *A Messerschmitt Bf 109E-7 on a desert airstrip* (Author's collection).

Below *Pilots of the 8th Staffel of 111/JG 2 hurriedly abandon their game of chess to scramble in their FW 190A-3s to intercept an Allied daylight raid. JG 2 was the Richthofen Geschwader* (Author's collection).

Far left *The 'Star of Africa', Hans-Joachim Marseille* (via Debbie George).

Left *Marseille was an accomplished pianist and is pictured at the keyboard with his mother* (via Debbie George).

Below left *Marseille's Bf 109F-4 (Trop). The trailing edge inboard flaps are clearly visible* (Author's collection).

Right *Heinz-Wolfgang Schnaufer, 'The Night Ghost of St Trond'* (via Norman Franks).

Below *An ace in the making? An unknown German pilot showing typical kill markings on the rudder of his Bf 109G* (Author's collection).

Above *Two Bf 110G-4a/R1 fighters of NJG 6 recorded in 1944. The aircraft are fitted with FuG 202 Lichtenstein BC radar, the aerials for which are on the nose (Author's collection).*

Below *Luftwaffe ace Ltn Joseph 'Sepp' Wurmheller of JG 2, Staffelkapitan of 9/JG 2. The aircraft is a FW 190A-5 with typical kill markings on the rudder (Author's collection).*

armoured version known as the *sturmjaeger*, the R8 (Ruestatz Field Conversion) comprising extra armour protection for the engine and pilot as well as two 30 mm Mk 108 cannon in the outer wing bays. This model normally had the twin MG 131 13 mm fuselage-mounted machine-guns removed, but Dahl insisted on their retention, so his fire-power was considerable.

The armour of the aircraft also afforded him tremendous protection from the 0.5 machine-guns of the American bombers and almost total immunity from the .303 rifle calibre defensive armament of British bombers. The equipment of this version of the FW 190 made it eminently suitable for attacking ground armour, so its effect on aluminium-skinned bombers can be imagined, and Dahl was a sufficiently skilled pilot to make maximum use of it. All his FW 190s carried a blue '13' on the fuselage which was more often than not outlined in white, and when he was Kommodore of *JG* 300 during the defence of the Reich the aircraft carried a blue/white/blue fuselage band.

Walther Dahl was born in Lug in 1916 and initially served with the infantry before transferring to the Luftwaffe and becoming a pilot, a capacity in which his natural ability quickly enabled him to become a top-rate fighter pilot. He served with *JG* 3 and was Geschwader Adjutant, a post that highlighted his administrative abilities and kept him from front-line action for long periods, hence his comparatively low final score of 128.

He flew in action over Malta, but it was on the Eastern Front that his marksmanship began to tell and in this theatre he achieved 77 victories, 25 of which were over Stalingrad during the winter of 1942-43. From July 1944, he served with *JG* 300 and by February 1945 reached his century. With the Luftwaffe putting up as strong a defence as was possible, he added 28 more before the final surrender, by which time he was an Oberst with the Ritterkreuz and Oak Leaves.

Dahl was a good all-round pilot and administrator, and probably typical of the backbone of most air forces. Circumstances prevented him reaching the top echelon of Luftwaffe aces, as far as total kills are concerned, but then similar circumstances also prevented many others from every air force from either achieving the heights or indeed surviving the war. It is appropriate perhaps simply to call it Fate.

ADOLF GALLAND

(LUFTWAFFE)

*W*ith the Battle of Britain over, the Luftwaffe retired to France to lick its wounds and prepare for the invasion of Russia, although in early 1941 few of its crews realized that Hitler was about to make such a misguided move. In England it was a period of consolidation, with new pilots, new aircraft and new tactics rejuvenating the RAF. Tentative sweeps late in 1940 increased in tempo in the early months of 1941, and by June these were increasing in scale as the war was carried across the Channel. On 21 June 1941, the eve of the German invasion of Russia, 23 Blenheims escorted by Spitfires flew a 'Circus' operation against the German airfield at St Omer.

It was now the German fighter pilots who were fighting with the 'home' advantage and no longer had duration and combat time limits enforced on them as they had in the previous summer over England. As the Blenheims mounted their attack, Bf 109s from *JG* 26 dived through the Spitfire screen and engaged them. The leader of the Bf 109s latched on to the tail of a bomber and soon saw smoke belching from it, followed by the crew taking to their parachutes. Turning his attention to a second bomber, he saw his bullets strike home then made the fatal mistake of watching it descend. Suddenly his world started to disintegrate around him as bullets from the escorting Spitfires crashed into his aircraft's cockpit and radiator. Instinctively, he threw the 109 into a violent evasive manoeuvre and escaped the attention of the British fighters, only for his engine to seize. Fortunately, he was able to force-land at the nearby Calais-Marck airfield and was taken by light aircraft back to *JG* 26's operational base from where he was flying again in the afternoon.

Once again he was in the thick of the fighting, this time with Spitfires over Boulogne, and again he made the classic mistake of following a victim down to watch it crash. This time he was not so lucky, for the Spitfire that now attacked him was flown by a man who knew his trade. Tracers crashed into the German fighter, tearing holes in the side and hitting the fuel tank. Splinters wounded the German pilot in the arms and head and he had the utmost difficulty in controlling his aircraft, but to his surprise he found the controls were still effective and noted that his altitude was 18,000 feet. At that moment the fuel tank exploded, and burning petrol cascaded over the aircraft. The pilot struggled to extricate himself from the wildly gyrating fighter and eventually by sheer strength and a very welcome element of luck he was thrown clear. He landed heavily in the Forest of Boulogne, had his wounds treated at a nearby field hospital and by nightfall was back with his unit.

One could be forgiven for thinking that the German pilot was a novice new to the front line and lucky to escape with his life after making two identical errors within hours of each other but he was not. The man concerned already had 69 victories to his credit and a Ritterkreuz with Oak Leaves; he was Major Adolf Galland, whose name is still a household word in aviation circles. Later the same day, the Blenheim he had hit in his morning combat was confirmed as crashing near St Omer, taking his score to 70. It was the only British bomber shot down on that occasion, so the other he had watched had returned safely to England. To cap an eventful day, he received notification of the addition of the Swords to his decorations.

His experiences on that June day illustrate how a moment's lapse can nearly cost a life, a situation that quite often happened to many aces. It was probably not for any reason of complacency or feeling of invincibility, but more likely fatigue that can cause even the best pilot to forget the basic rules he had instilled into his less experienced companions.

Galland was born in Westerhalt in March 1913 and his military career began in 1934 when he enlisted in *Infanterie Regiment* 10 in Dresden. Like many air-minded young Germans, Galland had first taken to the skies in a glider and soloed just after his seventeenth birthday. He went on to learn how to fly powered aircraft at one of the state-sponsored flying schools and later qualified for a commercial licence, being attached to Lufthansa before enlisting for military service.

He was commissioned in October 1934, and when the re-born Luftwaffe was announced to the world Galland was serving with *JG* 2 flying He 51 biplanes. He arrived in Spain in May 1937 to serve with 111/*J* 88, and flew the obsolete He 51 mainly on infantry support operations, completing nearly 300 missions before returning to Germany in July 1938 to work at the Air Ministry in Berlin. When war was declared on Poland, he returned to flying and during the three weeks of the Polish campaign flew 50 ground attack sorties in Henschel Hs 123s.

His ambition to fly fighters was finally realised in October 1939 when he joined *JG* 27 at Krefeld to fly Bf 109s. Up to this time he had not scored any aerial victories and had to wait until 10 May 1940 before he passed that landmark. He then made up for lost time with three Hurricanes in one day, and between then and 9 June he scored nine more victories to take his total to 12 at the start of the Battle of Britain. On 1 August his total stood at 17; he was awarded the Ritterkreuz, and became Kommodore of *JG* 26.

Six weeks later, he had underlined his skill as a fighter pilot with 23 more kills, taking his tally to 40, and by that fateful day in June when his career was so nearly ended, this had risen to 69. The following month, fate once again took a hand when some additional armour-plating, fitted on his own initiative by a member of his ground crew, took the full brunt of a 20 mm cannon shell which otherwise would have decapitated Major Galland. The rigger was given a cash reward and a period of leave whilst the fortunate pilot went on to achieve the greatest heights. These, however, also brought him problems of a different nature.

In November 1941 his great friend Moelders was killed in an air crash, and Galland was nominated to be his successor as Inspector General of Fighters. In December he was promoted to Oberst and in January 1942, with his personal score at 94, he was awarded the Diamonds to his Ritterkreuz with Swords and Oak Leaves. His rise to the heights of command increased steadily and in November of that year, at the age of 30, he became the youngest General in the German armed forces with the rank of Generalmajor. Galland was never frightened to stand up for his pilots and speak his mind – a dangerous thing for even a General to do in Nazi Germany – and this led to many confrontations with Goering. On one occasion, when the Reichsmarschall accused pilots of faking combat claims, Galland removed his decorations from his tunic, handed them to Goering and refused to wear them for a period of nearly a year.

In 1943 he returned to combat to see at first hand the new problems that were confronting his pilots as they fought the growing strength of the combined RAF and USAAC night and daylight raids. He became frustrated when Goering and others in authority would not listen to his logical analysis of the increasing problems that would face the diminishing resources of Germany and the Luftwaffe. Even after brushes with Mustangs and Thunderbolts in 1944, Goering would not believe him when he reported that the American bombers were being escorted all the way to and from their targets, so it is easy to imagine the increasing despondency felt by this talented leader.

He finally fell from grace in late 1944 when he violently opposed the planned New Year's Day operation against Allied airfields, claiming that the fighters involved would be better defending the Reich than trying to carry the fight to enemy airfields. The loss of over 300 German fighters on Operation Bodenplatte on 1 January 1945 probably proved his point. Although dismissed from his position of *General der Flieger*, his skills as a pilot were still highly regarded and in January he was ordered to gather the top Luftwaffe fighter pilots into one unit to fly the new jet-powered Me 262 into combat.

JV 44 was subsequently formed in February 1945 with a nucleus of 45 top pilots, of whom ten held the Ritterkreuz, and the majority were aces several times over. The jets proved Galland's point, made when he had watched the prototype fly in May 1943, that they could have brought havoc to the Allied air offensive had they been introduced a year earlier. Towards the end of March, the Me 262s were being equipped with air-to-air missiles, and these, together with their 30 mm cannons, made them as lethal as any fighter that was to serve in peace-time air forces for many years after the war. Galland scored at least seven kills in the Me 262 before being wounded by Mustangs on 26 April 1945.

Even with 104 kills to his credit, Galland was not among the top-scoring German aces, but it must be remembered that all his victories were against Commonwealth or American pilots, and for long periods he was not in combat situations. He served in the reformed Luftwaffe in 1956 and became highly respected among his former adversaries. He struck up firm and lasting friendships with the late Sir Douglas Bader, whom his *JG* 26 had shot down in 1941, the late Bob Stanford-Tuck and many other British aces and ordinary aircrew.

His leadership was superb and there can be little doubt that he was one of the greatest fighter pilots of the war. He was operational on the first and practically the last day of the conflict, flying a total of over 400 missions in addition to those flown in Spain.

ERICH HARTMANN

(LUFTWAFFE)

*T*he summer sun glinted on the cowling of the little Klemm two-seater as it turned off the downwind leg and lined up to land on the small grass strip at the club airfield near Stuttgart. It bounced slightly as its wheels kissed the ground, and soon it was moving towards a small boy who was eagerly awaiting his turn to fly in the passenger seat. A quick burst on the throttle swung the tail around, a boy jumped from the cockpit and the other took his place. Making sure that one son was clear and the other firmly strapped in, Frau Hartmann, wife of the local doctor, looked behind her and up, and, satisfied that all was clear, taxied out to the take-off point and was soon racing across the grass. The ride became smoother as the Klemm left the ground and a grin spread across her eight-year-old passenger's face as the thrill of being free of the earth heralded another Sunday afternoon's adventure.

It was 1930, and already young Erich Hartmann was acquiring the taste for adventure that had prompted his mother to buy a share in the light aircraft and spend most Sundays taking her sons joy-riding. Two years later, the economic crisis forced her to sell the aircraft but she never lost her feel for flying and, with the German public being encouraged to participate in every form of aviation, it was not long before she formed a gliding club at Weil, and naturally Erich took a leading role, eventually becoming an instructor in the Glider Group of the Hitler Youth.

As soon as he was 18 in April 1940, Erich applied to join the Luftwaffe; he was accepted and began his basic training in October. He made his first flight in a military aircraft at Gatow on 5 March 1941 and went solo three weeks later. By October he had completed his basic training and, after his advanced flying course and much to his delight, he was sent to the Fighter School at Zerbst near Magdeburg to convert to the Bf 109. Like many aces, Hartmann showed an early flair for gunnery but did not excel as a pilot; he had to concentrate really hard to ensure that his overall performance was good enough to bring the award of the coveted 'wings' which he received in March 1942. He was also commissioned as a Leutnant, and, on completion of all his training, was sent to join *JG* 52 operating on the Eastern Front.

He had hoped to ferry a new Bf 109 to the unit but one was not available, so he volunteered to take a Ju 87, an aircraft he had not flown before. It was reasoned that he was a pilot so should be able to fly any aircraft, but this was not so and to his consternation he crashed the dive-bomber on take-off. He completed the journey as a passenger in a Ju 52 and on arrival at his unit was assigned the task of flying as wing man to Stabsfeldwebel Eduard Rossman. With memories of the Ju 87 debacle still fresh in his mind, he took off for his first combat mission on 14 October 1942 – it nearly proved to be his last.

Although normally a rational and calm individual, he sometimes suffered from the exuberance of youth and, although on one occasion during training he had been grounded for unauthorized aerobatics, there was little sign that he would turn his first operation into such a near disaster. He and Rossman found a pair of Russian Il-2 ground attack aircraft and dived after them, but during the excitement of the chase Hartmann took his eyes off Rossman and the next thing he knew was that he was the centre of attraction for the Il-2s' fighter escorts. He managed to avoid the first pass then dived into the sanctuary of a nearby cloud; when he emerged the fighters had gone, but he spotted another diving at him. He hurled his Bf 109 all over the sky before pointing the nose to the west and, at full throttle, diving for home. Then the fuel warning light came on. With no idea where he was, he flew low until the 109's engine stopped, then crash-landed alongside a German convoy. He was taken the remaining 20 miles to his base by car where he received a frosty reception from Rossman, who had been the pilot diving to find him, and his CO, who was far from pleased at the loss of a Bf 109.

This was a far from encouraging start to his career as a fighter pilot, and at that time there was probably no-one on the unit who would have believed that during the next 2½ years he would become the highest-scoring ace of the war with 352 kills to his credit. His punishment was to work for three days with the ground crews, and during this time he reflected on his actions and resolved never to make the same mistakes again. When he did return to the cockpit, he stuck close to Rossman and learned from every move, analysing each one and working out better ways to get close to the enemy and be sure of a kill every time he fired his guns. His first victory came on 5 November 1942 when he shot down an Il-2, but the Russian managed to hit Hartmann who again was forced to crash-land and get home by courtesy of the German army. His first 100 sorties brought him only seven kills; by the time he had completed 200 trips in July 1943 his total had reached only 34.

The next two months saw him complete his third century of sorties which brought a dramatic rise in victories, his total now standing at 94. Immediately following his 90th victory on 19 August 1943 he was once again shot down, and was captured. Feigning injury, he managed to decoy his guards into not keeping as close a watch on him as they might, and when the truck in which he was travelling stopped to take cover from a strafing German aircraft, he seized his chance and bolted. Luckily he avoided contact with Russian patrols who would undoubtedly have killed him, and after several hours, including a spell when he helped an infantry unit repel a Russian attack, he once again got back to his unit.

He reached his century on 20 September 1943, and by March 1944 this had risen to 200. His reputation was now becoming widespread and the distinctive black arrow cowlings on his Bf 109 made him easily identifiable. There were few Russian pilots who wanted to meet the new Knight of Germany in the air, and eventually the markings were removed. Like his night-fighting contemporary – Heinz Schnaufer – multiple kills started to become commonplace. On one occasion, he destroyed the outer aircraft of a flight of four Il-2s with one burst, which caused it to blow up and take its three companions with it.

On 2 March 1944 he shot down ten aircraft in one day to celebrate the addition of the Oak Leaves to his Ritterkreuz. For a short period, *JG* 52 moved to Rumania to help counter the American daylight raids, and in two trips he shot down five P-51s. A Russian counter-offensive took the unit back to the Crimea and during May and June he accounted for 32 Russian aircraft to take his score to 282.

He was now vying with Major Gerhard Barkhorn for the top-scoring spot, then, with eight victories on 23 August, he passed the veteran pilot who had been flying in combat before the younger man had completed his training. By the end of August he reached 300 and became the 18th man to add the Diamonds to his Swords and Oak Leaves. In February he was given command of 1/*JG* 52 and on 8 May he shot down a Yak-11 which was his 352nd victory, and probably the last Luftwaffe kill of the Second World War. Within hours, Hartmann and his fellow pilots surrendered to an American armoured unit but were later handed over to the Russians.

Hartmann, who had flown 800 operational sorties, crashed 12 times and baled out once, was sentenced to 25 years hard labour by the Russians. He served ten years before being returned to Germany in 1955, and counted himself among the lucky ones as many of his companions never did return to their homeland. He served in the reformed Luftwaffe in 1956 and commanded *JG* 71, a Sabre-equipped fighter unit which carried the title 'Richthofen Geschwader'. There have been many claims that his score was exaggerated, but every one of his kills was verified by witnesses or his camera gun, so there is little doubt that Erich Hartmann will remain the top-scoring ace of all time.

HANS-JOACHIM JABS

(LUFTWAFFE)

*T*he Messerschmitt Bf 110 is a classic example of an aeroplane that has suffered from the widespread belief that it was a total failure. In fact, nothing could be further from the truth. Although it lacked the manoeuvrability and acceleration required to match the RAF's Spitfires and Hurricanes during the Battle of Britain, and its numbers were decimated whilst trying to carry out its original design role as a long-range escort fighter, it proved to be an ideal interim night fighter, and in this role it was so successful that it was developed into the backbone of the Luftwaffe's night fighter force.

At the beginning of the Second World War, neither the RAF nor Luftwaffe had given a great deal of thought to night fighting, but by the end both had radar-equipped, heavily armed, long-range aircraft capable of carrying out night fighting as well as intruder work. The story of the development of night fighting is a fascinating one, and in its telling the names of many aces from both sides appear. Many of these pilots were specialists who achieved great success purely as night fighter pilots, but there are also those who learned their trade the hard way, and when they started their careers never dreamed that they would become hunters under the cover of darkness.

One such ace was the German pilot Hans-Joachim Jabs who joined the Luftwaffe just one month after his nineteenth birthday in December 1936. His initial training as a fighter pilot was on Bf 109s, but like many others he was transferred to the heavy twin Bf 110 and joined 11/*ZG* 76 in time to fly offensive patrols over France and escort sorties over England. However, unlike many of his companions he survived the air battles over England and the Channel and emerged as the top-scoring Bf 110 pilot during this period, with 19 kills which included at least 12 single-seater British fighters.

Recognition of his prowess came with the award of the Ritterkreuz on 1 October 1940. 11/*ZG* 76 was one of the units that suffered during the Battle, and it was withdrawn to be re-trained as a night fighter unit, eventually adopting this mantle in November 1941 when it became fully operational as 111/*NJG* 3. It was nearly seven months later that Jabs scored the first of his night victories when he shot down a Stirling in late June 1942, following this in July with a Wellington.

One of the originators of the night fighter force was Hauptmann Helmet Lent, and it was his unit, 1V/NJG 1, that Jabs joined at Leeuwarden in November 1942. Lent's squadron was equipped with Bf 110F-4s which carried the *Lichtenstein* C-1 interception equipment, and on 17 December Jabs and his radar operator put this to good use when they shot down a Halifax and a Stirling. Two more victories were recorded in January 1943, then on 4 February Jabs led eight aircraft from his unit into combat with B-17s during an early daylight raid. The Bf 110s, which were deadly at night when they were able to stalk their victims, proved to be something of a handful in action against the heavily armed American bombers, and although Jabs shot down a B-17, all eight Bf 110s were damaged to a greater or lesser extent.

As radar interception and corresponding countermeasures tipped the scales one way and then the other, the night initiative gradually passed to the defending fighters. The RAF's night bombers with their .303 Browning machine-guns were no match for a well-flown Bf 110, for although the speed differential was marginal, speed was by no means the main criterion. Most German night fighter aces agree that they looked out for bombers that appeared to be unaware of their presence. If, as they approached, the bomber started to take evasive action, the experienced night fighter crew would usually break off the engagement and look for easier prey. The cannon-armed Bf 110s could stay well outside the range of the RAF's multi-engined bombers' machine-guns, and it is perhaps somewhat ironic to consider that if the bombers had not had to carry two heavy turrets complete with guns and ammunition, the weight saved might well have given them enough speed advantage to make interception by Bf 110s difficult. As it was, there were of course problems, but on the whole the night fighter losses due to enemy bombers were fairly low; for example, in one 17-month period, 1V/*NJG* 1 suffered no combat losses.

Jabs' successes at night continued on 19 February with a hat-trick of Stirlings, and two months later, on 9 April, he shot down the first of the ten Lancasters that were to fall to his guns. His most successful month was June 1943 when he accounted for six bombers, and on 1 August he took over command of 1V/*NJG* 1 from Lent. The award of the Oak Leaves to his Ritterkreuz came in March 1944, the same month that he took over from Werner Streib as Kommodore of *NJG* 1, a position he was to hold until the cessation of hostilities.

Oddly enough, his narrowest escape did not come at the hands of an alert bomber crew but from pilots of the first type of British aircraft he had met in combat back in 1940, the Spitfire. On 29 April 1944, he was in the approach configuration in his Bf 110G-4 at Arnhem-Deelen when he was bounced by two sections of Spitfire IXs. With superb airmanship, Jabs avoided the first pass and in so doing hit one of the Spitfires with his 30 mm cannon as it overshot – his 46th victory. He then almost immediately repeated the dose to score his 47th. Meanwhile, the remaining six British fighters recovered their composure, and proved more than a match for the heavy 110, damaging it so badly that Jabs was forced to crash-land and quickly evacuate the wreck and the Spitfires reduced it to scrap.

Three more Lancasters fell to his cannons before his war ended on 21 February 1945. Like many other Luftwaffe pilots, he fought throughout the war, during which he flew 710 operational sorties and scored 50 victories of which 28 were at night. His score does not place him in the top echelon of Luftwaffe night fighter aces, for although he was a more than capable pilot he was not outstanding. It is probably true to say that he was a typical example of the type of man who found night fighting to his liking, and was reasonably successful without being too adventurous or flamboyant.

HELMUT LENT

(LUFTWAFFE)

On 18 December 1939, the German naval radar station on Heligoland and the Luftwaffe Freya installation on the island of Wangerooge detected a large formation of hostile aircraft approaching at a range of 113 kilometres. Lt Hermann Diehl, in charge of the Freya, immediately advised the Luftwaffe fighter Gruppen co-ordination centre, but at this stage of the war communications were poor, and Diehl was always being questioned as to whether or not his 'new-fangled' gadgets had picked up a genuine sighting or just a formation of seagulls. Consequently there was a 20-minute delay before Bf 110s and Bf 109s from Jever and Wangerooge were scrambled.

Among the crews of the Bf 110s of 1/*ZG* 76 was Ltn Helmut Lent, who on the opening day of the Polish campaign had destroyed several bombers on the ground and on the second day a PZL 11c in the air. He now sat patiently in the cockpit of his Bf 110 with his radio operator, Unteroffizier Kubisch, and armourer Oberfeldwebel Mahle, struggling to complete the loading of a drum of 20 mm ammunition. The armourer had just secured the clips and was sliding off the wing when the order to take off came. Lent gunned the Bf 110 into action, but even as he took to the air the RAF Wellingtons that Diehl had reported could be seen as they headed for Wilhelmshaven; the warning gained by the radar had already been forfeited.

As it turned out, it was not of great importance since the British bombers were no match for the Bf 109s and 110s. Lent saw the main point of the fighters' attack taking place north of Wangerooge, but as he turned to join the melee he spotted a pair of Wellingtons creeping off to the west. Lent knew that the bombers were equipped with a rear turret armed with four Browning rifle calibre machine-guns, and he also knew that the cross-fire from two bombers could be dangerous. So, taking his time, he moved his aircraft into a spot above and to the beam of the bombers which could not be reached by their gunners.

Choosing his moment, he dived on to the Wellingtons and was surprised when after just a short burst from his guns, the rear aircraft burst into flames; the pilot managed to gain some sort of control and crash-landed on the island of Borkum. Meanwhile, Lent set off after the other aircraft and caught up with it as it wave-hopped in a frantic bid to reach safety. Once again, a burst from the Bf 110 was enough to set the Wellington's fuel tanks (which were not self-sealing) on fire, and the aircraft plunged into the sea, breaking up as it hit the water. Overjoyed at his success, Lent headed home, but on the way encountered another damaged Wellington and administered the *coup de grâce*.

This costly lesson for the RAF taught it that daylight bombing was not possible even with the theoretical protection of combined fire-power, and the seeds were laid for the future night offensive. In Germany it strengthened Goering's view that bombers would not fly over the Reich, and among the fighter pilots there was a firmly held belief that the war would not last long. However, Ernst Udet had pre-warned Goering that he should have a night fighter force just in case, and on his insistence a handful of Arado 68s and Bf 109s had been co-operating with searchlight units in a token gesture. The action on 18 December involved several day fighter pilots including Johannes Steinhof, Werner Streib, Victor Moelders (brother of Werner) and Lent, who were all to become night fighter aces, despite their reluctance in 1940-41 to join the embryo night fighter force.

Lent achieved ace status during the Norwegian campaign when he shot down the Norwegian air force Gladiator of Sgt Per Schye. Soon after this, he and Kubisch had a narrow escape when they tore the undercarriage off their Bf 110 as they landed at Oslo-Fornebu whilst it was still being stoutly defended by Norwegian ground forces. Lent was greatly disappointed when he was posted to command the 6th Staffel of 11/*NJG* 1, and initially could not come to terms with the different technique of night fighting, wherein patience and the ability to stalk the foe until in a position of advantage were greatly different to the cut-and-thrust of the dogfight.

Eventually, after two dozen sorties without success, he sought an interview with Major Falck, the Kommodore of *NJG* 1, and requested a return to day fighters, his reason being that he could not see at night! Falck rejected the request and in so doing sealed the fate of 102 bomber crews. Lent strived for success and finally, on the night of 11-12 May 1941, on his 35th sortie, he finally brought down two Wellingtons.

Success now followed success, and by the end of the year 18 more bombers, including his first two four-engined types, both Stirlings, had become his victims. Throughout 1942, now proudly wearing a Ritterkreuz to which the Oak Leaves were added in June, he roamed the night skies steadily adding to his total; a Halifax on 18 January 1943 brought him the honour of being the first night fighter pilot to score 50 victories. His next aim was to be the first to the magic century, and by July 1943 he had scored 65 among which was his first Mosquito. The following month he added the Swords to his decorations, and was promoted to the command of *NJG* 3.

His century was reached on the night of 15-16 June 1944 when three Lancasters were brought down, and by the end of July he became the first night fighter ace to reach 100 night victories. This brought the award of the Diamonds, making him the first night fighter pilot to be so recognized.

Oberstleutnant Lent has been credited with the invention of the infamous vertically firing cannons *(Schräge Musik)* that were fitted to many German night fighters and created havoc among British bombers, but this weapon was the work of Paul Mahle, an armourer who, in 1939, had been unceremoniously dumped off the wing of Lent's Bf 110 as he hurried to take off in pursuit of the Wellingtons, so there is a tenuous connection between the two men!

On 5 October 1944, Lent was landing his Bf 110 at Paderborn when an engine cut out and, in trying to regain height on only one, he hit a power cable. The ace with 110 kills to his name survived the crash, which killed his crew, but two days later he succumbed to his injuries. Thus died a reluctant night fighter pilot who ended up with the second highest score in that arena.

HANS-JOACHIM MARSEILLE

(LUFTWAFFE)

*T*he strains of the Wedding March echoed from the small country church as the smiling bride and groom walked into the afternoon sunshine and the bells started to peel as guests and relatives waited to greet the newly-weds. Suddenly the tranquillity of the scene was shattered by the roar of a low-flying fighter aircraft, which dived on the church, circled the steeple then, in a series of upward spirals, climbed into the azure blue sky. A salute to the happy couple from a friend? No, it was just one of the occasions that the young pilot of the Bf 109 could not resist – to him, church steeples seemed to represent a challenge, as did uncompleted *autobahns* on which he often sent workmen skurrying for cover as he practised approaches and landings.

This irresponsible attitude was one of the factors that nearly brought an end to the career of a Luftwaffe pilot who was to become the highest-scoring ace against the Allies, a man who was to cover himself in glory in the Western Desert and become universally known to friend and foe alike as '*Der Stern von Afrika*' (the Star of Africa). He was Hauptmann Hans-Joachim Marseille.

Marseille inherited his love of aeroplanes from his father, General Siegfried Marseille, a First World War pilot of Hugenot ancestry who was to die commanding a Luftwaffe unit in Russia in 1943. Hans-Joachim was born on 13 December 1919 at Charlottenburg, Berlin, but whilst he was still very young his mother and father divorced. Thus, the firm hand of discipline which was a hallmark of his strict Prussian father, was missing in his formative years, and may account for the young Joachim's free-spirited pranks.

On completion of his formal education, he joined the Luftwaffe on 11 July 1938 and began his flying training on 7 November under the guiding hand of First World War Austro-Hungarian ace Julius Arigi (32 kills) at Jagdfliegerschule Wein-Schwechat. Despite his antics and apparent lack of respect for his seniors, he successfully completed his course and was posted as an Oberfahnrich (officer cadet) to 3/1/*LG* 2 to gain combat experience. His first victory came on his third sortie when he shot down a Spitfire, and by the end of the Battle of Britain he had seven scores to his name. However, on the debit side he had been shot down four times, on one occasion being forced to bale out into the Channel, an incident that coloured his thinking about the use of parachutes and made him much prefer to attempt crash-landing whenever possible.

During this period he had graduated from *LG* 2 to Johannes Steinhoff's 1V/*JG* 52, but his record was such that eventually Steinhoff, who was to become a top ace with 176 kills and end the war flying Me 262s, decided that the young pilot was too much of a liability. In January 1941, he had him transferred to *JG* 27 at Döberitz near Berlin. Marseille's cavalier attitude and love of parties generated a playboy image that made the handsome blond pilot very popular in some quarters, but very unpopular in others. On joining *JG* 27, he was assigned to the third Staffel under the command of Hauptmann Gerhard Homuth, with whom Marseille very quickly clashed. Homuth stood no nonsense from the young cadet, and on one occasion, when he refused to assign a combat mission to Marseille, the future ace took off and strafed the ground close to Homuth's tent, an action for which he was lucky not to have been court-martialled.

In April 1941, the unit was moved to North Africa and set up camp with its Bf 109Es at Gazala. During the move from Tripoli to the base on 22 April, Marseille's aircraft developed engine trouble and he was forced to land in the desert. He hitched a lift with an Italian supply truck and on arrival at a supply depot arrogantly demanded transport to his unit, telling the commanding officer that he was a Flight Commander and must get back immediately. The senior German officer knew very well that the young pilot facing him was in fact only an Oberfahnrich, but admired his cheek and rewarded his initiative with the loan of an Opel Admiral and driver.

The following day, Marseille shot down a Hurricane over Tobruk and followed this five days later with a Blenheim, although once again his own aircraft was seriously damaged in the fights. Homuth continually lectured the young pilot about his airmanship, and eventually referred him to the Gruppen Kommanduer Eduard Neumann, who could see the pilot's potential and decided to act as his mentor. This move was fundamental in setting Marseille on the right track, and from then on he started to concentrate on developing his skills.

He was a master of the deflection shot and worked hard on tactics, which he practised on his luckless companions as they returned from patrols. It all paid off, however, and during the next month his score had risen to 14 and at last his commission was confirmed. Marseille's reputation spread through the desert and later his sand-camouflaged Bf 109s which carried a yellow '14' (his call-sign) on the fuselage, were as familiar as von Richthofen's red Triplane had been. Another interesting insight to his character is that he chose a young African named Matthias as his batman, and soon the two became firm friends without losing respect for each other.

Marseille's basic character did not change, and his quarters in the desert were still often the scenes of parties at which Matthias would set up and tend a makeshift bar in an extension to his master's living quarters. When *JG* 27 moved to a new location at Derna in December 1941, Joachim's score had reached 40 and he was beginning to cultivate a taste for multiple victories. His 50th came on 24 February 1942, two days after he had been awarded his Ritterkreuz.

In April he was promoted to Oberleutnant, and took over command of the third Staffel from Homuth, who in turn took over I Gruppe when Neumann became Geschwader Kommodore. Both men had played a major part in seeing the new ace adopt a more responsible attitude towards discipline, which had enabled him to accept his own command, and had undoubtedly saved his life by making him take a close look at his airmanship. Then, just as he began to enjoy his new command, a personal tragedy hit him. His young sister Inge, to whom Joachim was very close, died in mysterious circumstances in Vienna. This was a blow from which Marseille never recovered, and he sought solace in the tranquillity of his tent playing jazz music, and vengeance in the skies over the desert.

On 17 June he scored six in one day, flying a new 'F' version of the Bf 109, a model he came to love, and with his score at 101 Neumann sent him home to rest. He was now a legendary figure in Germany and was fêted wherever he went. The award of his Swords and Oak Leaves followed, and he also received from the hands of Mussolini the Italian Gold Medal for Bravery, recognition indeed, since Erwin Rommel only ever received the same award in silver.

He returned to North Africa on 23 August 1942 and, flying a new Bf 109F, carried on from where he had left off. The achievement for which he is probably best remembered came on 1 September. Taking off at 07.30 to escort JU 87s, he spotted ten Kittyhawks approaching just as the dive-bombers began their attack. In the space of two minutes he shot down two of the fighters, then, as the Ju 87s withdrew, he accounted for another. On the way back to base, his flight was intercepted by Spitfires and during the next nine minutes six of them had fallen to Marseille's guns. On landing at 09.14, his armourer found that he had used just 20 cannon shells and 60 rounds of machine-gun ammunition to down nine aircraft. That day he flew two more sorties and shot down another eight aircraft, including five P-40s in the space of six minutes. His total of 17 in one day was only beaten once, by Emil Lang on the Russian Front.

The following day it was announced that Marseille would be presented with his Diamonds personally by the Führer in the autumn, but fate was to decree otherwise and neither he, nor his family, ever received them. His joy was tempered by sad news on 5 September when his best friend, 'Fifi' Stahlschmidt (59 kills), was killed. Marseille became increasingly withdrawn and morose, and although he added 26 more victories to his total by the end of the month, his overall condition caused some concern among his friends.

On the morning of Wednesday 30 September he took off with Oblts Schlang and Poettgen to carry out a sweep in the Cairo area. Marseille was flying a new 'G' model Bf 109 and, on returning from the uneventful patrol at a height of about 4,500 feet, a glycol line broke and set the oil cooler on fire. As his cockpit filled with smoke, he opened the small windscreen ventilator to clear it. This had little effect, and his companions pleaded with him over their radios to bale out. However, the trio of Bf 109s were still three minutes flying time away from the safety of the German lines, and Marseille had no desire to become a PoW. The cockpit continued to fill with acrid smoke, preventing him seeing or breathing properly; his wing man tried to guide him, but it became obvious that the 109 was doomed.

As soon as the trio crossed the line, Marseille flicked his aircraft on to its back, jettisoned the canopy and tried to drop clear, but he had not realized that the aircraft was in a nose-down attitude and centrifugal force held him firmly in place. He eventually struggled free, but as he fell was knocked unconscious by a massive blow to the left side of his chest from the fin that carried the 158 kill markings. He never recovered to deploy his parachute and fell to his death four miles south of Sidi Abdul Rahman.

At his funeral on 2 October in the cemetery at Derna, Neumann said, 'A restless heart is now resting, but we fly on. May the fighting spirit of Marseille inspire all men of *JG* 27'. His final score included 101 Curtiss Tomahawks and Kittyhawks, 30 Hurricanes, 16 Spitfires and four bombers. Adolf Galland was moved to call him 'the unrivalled virtuoso among fighter pilots of the Second World War'. The simple plaque erected over his grave by the pilots of *JG* 27 was perhaps the most fitting epitaph of all: 'Here lies undefeated Hauptmann Hans Marseille'.

WERNER MOELDERS

(LUFTWAFFE)

On 20 September 1940, ten Spitfires of No 92 Sqn airborne from Biggin Hill are circling at 5,000 feet over Gravesend waiting to link up with No 41 Sqn. The ground controller is advised of an incoming raid and instructs the British fighters to climb to Angels 20 (20,000 feet) to intercept this. At approximately 11.30, the leader of the British formation is instructed to turn south and climb to 27,000 feet. As the fighters struggle to gain height, Messerschmitt Bf 109s flying in formations of four, descend from the sun and soon the Spitfire pilots are fighting for their lives.

The leader of the Bf 109s, with his wing man clinging to his tail like a limpet, selects two Spitfires which are soon spinning down. Plt Off H. P. Hill crashes near Folkestone and Sgt P. R. Eyles falls into the Channel. Both men, who only joined No 92 on 1 July, are killed, the 39th and 40th victims of the leader of *JG* 51, Werner Moelders, who on the following day was awarded the Oak Leaves to his Knights' Cross. Moelders was one of the highest-calibre German pilots to emerge from the Second World War; not only was he a superb pilot, but was also a remarkable tactician and innovator who is generally considered to be the 'father' of fighter tactics adopted by the Luftwaffe during the war, hence his nickname 'Vati' (Daddy).

Moelders had a burning ambition to be a soldier, but in 1923 an uncle took him on a pleasure flight and from then on his sole ambition was to fly. Overcoming initial problems of air sickness and disorientation, he was one of the first pilots to enlist in Hitler's secret Luftwaffe, becoming an instructor before moving to Spain to command 3 Staffel of *J* 88 of the Legion Kondor when it converted to the Bf 109C from the He 51.

It was during this conflict that he devised the 'finger four' system in which fighters flew in two pairs (Rottes) that formed a four section flight (Schwarm). This formation, in which each pair covered the tails of the others, gave a tremendous measure of flexibility and was to be adopted by the Allies when their own pre-war methods of V formations with a 'tail-end Charlie' acting as a weaver proved disastrous.

By the time the Second World War was declared, Moelders was the Legion's leading ace with 14 victories to his credit, and by the end of 1939 he had added four more to this total. During the so-called 'Phoney War', which ended on 10 May 1940, he commanded 111/*JG* 53 and added six more to his total, which a month later had risen to 15, making him the top Luftwaffe scorer for the period. This was a remarkable achievement bearing in mind the few actions he was involved in, together with the fact that after being shot down by a French Dewoitine 520 on 5 June he spent two uncomfortable weeks as a PoW. Nonetheless, even without the Spanish victories he was fêted as the top Luftwaffe ace and received the Ritterkreuz from a grateful Führer.

During the Battle of Britain he commanded *JG* 51 and was involved in a three-way unofficial competition with Adolf Galland and Helmut Wick to see who could outscore the other. On 22 October he became the first of the trio to reach his half century, then had a barren period during which Wick overtook him before being killed in combat with RAF ace 'Cocky' Dundas and the Spitfires of No 609 Sqn during November. His next ten victories were slow in coming, taking him until February 1941, by which time he was flying the improved 'F' version of the Bf 109, to reach 60.

On 22 June, he was in the forefront of the fighting during the invasion of Russia and on that day accounted for four Soviet aircraft. The same month his score passed 80, thus taking him beyond the legendary von Richthofen, and by the end of the month his total stood at 96. The big question now was, would he be the first Second World War Luftwaffe pilot to reach the magic century? His Spanish victories did in fact take him beyond this landmark, but they were not taken into account at this stage. Nonetheless, two confirmed scores on 15 July took his total to 101 (115 overall), at which point he was forbidden to fly on operations.

This was an interesting situation that rarely occurred later in the war when the Luftwaffe was very short of experienced fighter pilots and allowed most of them to fly on until they were killed, captured, or seriously injured. The award of Diamonds to the Swords of the Ritterkreuz was made on 15 July 1941, and at the age of 28 he was promoted to *Oberst* and appointed to the post of Inspector of Fighters.

On 22 November 1941, he was a passenger in a He 111 taking him to Ernst Udet's funeral when the aircraft crashed on landing at Breslau and he was killed. Although by comparison with some other Luftwaffe aces his score was not outstanding, he would clearly have achieved similar heights if he had lived to see further action. As it happened, his memory was, and still is, perpetuated by *JG* 51 which was given the name 'Moelders' to honour his memory.

WALTER OESAU

(LUFTWAFFE)

*F*or every extrovert ace whose deeds and actions attracted the limelight, there are many who neither sought nor wanted such attentions,
but by their overall ability as leaders and skilled flyers achieved success
that has ensured them a different type of recognition in the annals of
aviation.

Such a man was Oberst Walter Oesau, the son of a bank director who
fought with the Legion Kondor in Spain, and on the Western and Eastern
fronts until May 1944 when, like many of his generation, he was killed in
action. Known to his friends as 'Gulle', he learned to fly with the reborn
Luftwaffe in the 1930s and on completing his training joined the Jagdges-
chwader 'Richthofen'. He was one of the first fighter pilots to join *J* 88 in
Spain where he gained eight victories and became one of only 27 recipients
of the Spanish Cross with Diamonds. He was also wounded in this
campaign, and throughout the rest of his career wore the Spanish Wound
Badge on his left breast close to his Iron Cross First Class.

When the war in the west started he was with 111/*JG* 51, and by 22
August had become the second Luftwaffe pilot to reach 20 Second World
War victories, bringing him the award of a Ritterkreuz. His prowess was
such that by February 1941 he had doubled this score and earned himself
the Oak Leaves to his Ritterkreuz, only the fourth Luftwaffe pilot to be so
honoured at this time.

Oesau's talents were not only in combat flying, for he was also a born
leader and understood the many different types of personalities that
combined to form a typical fighter squadron, as well as being capable of
moulding these into an efficient fighting force. It was no surprise, therefore,
when he moved with *JG* 51 to the Eastern Front when the invasion of
Russia was launched. In one outstanding month in Russia he scored 44
victories, including a run of 16 in as many days, and on one occasion shared
in the destruction of seven Soviet fighters with another pilot in the space of
20 minutes. There can be little doubt that such prolific scoring would have
taken him much higher in the overall list of aces if he had stayed in that
theatre.

However, fate, which so often contrived to curtail such high scoring
activity, now selected 'Gulle' and at the end of July he was called back to the

west to take over the command of *JG* 2, where his special style of leadership was required as the Allied offensive gathered momentum. On 15 July, his victory tally had reached 78 and he became only the third man to be awarded the newly instituted Swords which were personally presented to him by Hitler. His next target was a century of kills, and this was reached in October with the destruction of a Spitfire. He became only the third Luftwaffe pilot to reach such a landmark, but once again fate stepped in and he was forbidden to fly further combat missions, his experience in both flying and the art of leadership being considered too valuable to risk.

A series of staff appointments meant that many other less talented leaders overtook his score, but in October 1943 events were beginning to thwart Hitler's ambitions, and Oesau's skill was required in the front line. He took command of *JG* 1 on 8 October when Oberstlt Hans Philip (201 kills) was killed, and soon showed that he had lost none of his skills, scoring at least ten victories against the formidable American box formations of B-17s and B-24s.

In May 1944 it was the USAAC that brought Oesau's downfall. He was flying a combat patrol near the Eiffel mountains when a P-38 caught him by surprise, and before he could take effective evasive action he was trapped by the twin-engined American fighter. On this occasion there was no escape, and Walter Oesau, a true gentleman and a gallant pilot, paid the ultimate price.

PRINCE HEINRICH zu SAYN-WITTGENSTEIN

(LUFTWAFFE)

At the beginning of the Second World War, night fighting was very much an area that had been neglected by both sides. When it was realized that even in daylight heavily armed bombers without fighter escorts were virtually sitting targets, and night bombing started to be developed, the need for an effective fighter force capable of operating in darkness with electronic aids became increasingly apparent. The advancement of airborne interception equipment, countermeasures, ground control, tactics and armaments in this field was probably greater in the 5½ years of the European war than any other type of equipment or fighting technology during the same period.

The Luftwaffe was very quick to develop a system of small 'boxes' of monitored air space which were retaining in their basic form from 1941 until the end of the war, operational methods and control systems being modified as the need arose. By mid-1943, RAF Bomber Command losses were gradually mounting as the radar-equipped and controlled night fighters were directed into the main bomber stream or patrolled the edges looking for stragglers. On 24-25 July 1943, the British at last decided to use a countermeasure they had developed but previously hesitated in employing as they feared it would be copied and used in return. This was the dropping of strips of foil 27 cms long and 2 cms wide that gave the same signal on ground and airborne radar as a bomber. The code name for this was 'Window', and the first target to be chosen to be bombed under its cover was Hamburg. The result was beyond belief, and the night fighters were thrown into total chaos.

However, by the end of the year the Germans had introduced a suitable counter and the pendulum started to swing their way again; but in the electronics war events moved quickly, and it was not too long before another simple counter was devised. This was the introduction of German-speaking personnel operating from transmitters in England and broadcasting fake messages to Luftwaffe night fighter crews. Code-named 'Corona', this was introduced on 22 October 1943 in a raid on Kassel, and once again frustrated night fighter crews. However, the latter soon found that the tail warning radar being fitted to British bombers, 'Fishpond', emitted a signal that they could home in on. Nonetheless, there can be little doubt that many of these devices saved bomber crews who might otherwise have fallen to the guns of night fighters, but they also produced nervousness in some cases and over-confidence in others.

On the night of 21 January 1944, Bomber Command was briefed to attack Magdeburg. 'Window' and all the other devices had brought an appreciable drop in the loss rate during the last five months of 1943, and those crews due to carry out this raid could be forgiven for thinking that maybe the Luftwaffe night fighter force was in some disarray. German ground controllers plotted the incoming raid and from its track assumed that the target was to be Hamburg again. They therefore ordered their main force to head for this area, leaving the night fighters' marshalling point at beacon Quelle, located between Cuxhaven and Hamburg, free when the main bomber stream thundered over it and turned towards Magdeburg. The 'spoof' raid, planned to create the decoy which a nervous ground controller had fallen for, worked perfectly, but some target markers, falling well to the south, were seen by fighter crews who ignored the order to orbit Hamburg and headed for the fires.

Among these was the *Geschwader Kommodore* of *NJG* 2, Major Prince Heinrich zu Sayn-Wittgenstein, and his radar operator, Feldwebel Ostheimer, who had taken off from Stendal at 2100 hours in Ju 88C-6c *R4 + XM*. Their mission was a *Zahme Sau* (Tame Boar) patrol, which meant that they would be guided into the bomber stream then use the aircraft's radar to find individual targets. The Prince and his operator were masters at this, and as the Ju 88 they were flying had the latest Lichtenstein SN-2 radar, their hopes were high. The speed of the Ju 88 took them to the area quickly and, about an hour after take-off, Ostheimer picked up a target.

The night fighter homed in on what turned out to be a Lancaster, and soon it was plunging earthwards in flames. The fighter then climbed back towards the bomber stream and soon the radar set was swamped with echoes; at least six targets were within reach, and once again Ostheimer guided his pilot to another unsuspecting Lancaster which met the same fate as its fellow. Two more Lancasters were shot down in the sortie, the fourth meeting its end just 40 minutes after the first.

At this point the Prince's score stood at 83, making him the Luftwaffe's top-scoring night fighter ace. The Ju 88 continued its patrol and soon a fifth bomber was detected; the Prince opened fire and saw strikes on the fuselage, but as he closed in for the kill there was a tremendous explosion, the night fighter started to shake and the port wing burst into flames. Wittgenstein jettisoned the canopy and told Ostheimer to bale out. The radar operator tore off his helmet and dived out of the burning Junkers, landing safely near Schoenhausen, but Wittgenstein could not get out of the crashing night fighter and his body was found in the wreckage the following day.

So died a man who, like many other successful night fighter pilots, had started his career in an entirely different branch of the Luftwaffe. Born on 14 August 1916 in Copenhagen, Wittgenstein joined the Wehrmacht in 1936 but transferred to the Luftwaffe and became a bomber pilot with *KG* 1 and *KG* 51. In the spring of 1942, he re-trained on night fighters and by the end of the year was Staffelkapitan of 9/*NJG* 2. His first victory came on 2 March 1942 when he shot down a Blenheim, and by October his tally stood at 20. At the end of 1942 he was ordered to help defend Ostpreussen against Russian bombers, and flew with 1V/*NJG* 5 from Insterburg where, between 16 April and 2 May 1943, he added five Russian bombers to his tally. With the Allied night bombing on the increase he returned to Holland where, in just under a month, he claimed five RAF bombers. He then returned to Orel where once again he was in action against the Russian bombing offensive.

Most of his missions were flown in the Ju 88 which in a variety of forms proved to be one of the Luftwaffe's most successful night fighters. He loved to fly this aircraft on what he often called *Expressjaeger* (fast hunter) sorties in which the speed of the aircraft enabled him to operate very effectively within an 80 km radius of a Himmelbet radar station. This type of mission brought him several multiple kills, including six on the night the RAF first used 'Window' over Hamburg (24-25 July 1943). It also brought about his downfall just six months later when, on the night already described, he fell victim to a Mosquito, which, like the Ju 88 the Prince was flying, had started on the designer's board as a bomber, and ended the war as a successful 'Jack of all trades', and master of most of them.

On the night in question the RAF lost 55 bombers, a sobering thought for those commanders who had started to think the falling loss rate indicated a decline in the night fighter defence. The Luftwaffe lost four night fighters, but two of them were flown by top aces: Wittgenstein and Manfred Meurer (65 kills). The Prince's final score of 83 – at least 28 were Russians – made him the third highest scoring night fighter pilot in the Luftwaffe. He received the Ritterkreuz after his 40th victory, the Oak Leaves were added after his 64th and finally he was awarded the Swords on the day following his death.

HEINZ SCHNAUFER

(LUFTWAFFE)

*W*hilst Jabs and Lent were somewhat reluctant convertees from day to night fighting, the same cannot be said of the man who was to survive the war as Germany's top night fighter ace with a total of 121 night victories, and a Ritterkreuz with Diamonds, Swords and Oak Leaves. Heinz-Wolfgang Schnaufer took to night fighting like the proverbial duck to water, and joined 11/*NJG* 1 immediately after completing his training.

The 20-year-old Leutnant had all the attributes of a top-class night fighter pilot, and these soon became evident on the night of 2 June 1942 when he recorded his first kill. At this time the Germans had devised the simple but effective system of dividing their airspace into boxes, each of which was patrolled by night fighters that were warned of the approach of enemy bombers by ground radar interpreted by a ground controller. Once the aircraft had entered the 'box', the night fighter used its on-board radar to track it and hopefully shoot it down. Throughout the war, this system was improved and revised as both sides found counters for the other's new equipment, but generally it always ended with the fighter crew being the last link between the bomber and its fate.

The long loiter time of aircraft like the Bf 110, Ju 88 and later the He 219, enabled the crews to intercept the RAF night bomber streams over very long distances, and there were many occasions when bomber crews relaxed their vigils just that little bit too soon and paid the ultimate price. Of course, it required a considerable amount of fortitude and self-discipline to stay alert at the controls of a heavy fighter for several hours, listening to the ground controller, the aircraft's radar operator, and peering into the darkness to spot tell-tale flames from exhausts or the sudden burst of fire as another night fighter made an interception. Some crews flew several months without victories and some were content with downing one bomber then relaxing their own vigil.

Schnaufer was exceptional, and his record of multiple kills was not matched by any other night ace. This skill came to light on the night of 16 December 1943 when, in extremely poor weather conditions, he persisted with his patrol and shot down four Lancasters. At this time his score stood at 36, of which 22 had been achieved by the previous August when he became Staffelkapitan of 9/1V/*NJG* 1. This promotion seemed to act as a spur, for in the next four months he added 14 more before his first multiple victory. Before the end of 1943 he scored twice more to reach 42, at which point he was awarded the Ritterkreuz.

In early 1944 he reached the ranks of the half-centurians in a gallop with nine Lancasters, six of which fell to him on two nights. Multiple kills became an everyday occurrence as the fine spring weather made conditions ideal for the fighters, and disastrous for the bombers. April brought him nine more Lancasters, four on the 27th alone, and in May nine more together with four Halifaxes fell to his guns, three of the latter being shot down on the 13th and no fewer than five of the former on 24th. It is not surprising that promotion as well as decorations followed at a swift rate, and when he became only the second night fighter pilot to achieve 100 victories on 9 October, he was already the Kommandeur of 1V/*NJG* 1; by the end of 1944, his score stood at 106, which took him ahead of his nearest rival, Helmut Lent.

However, his greatest achievement was yet to come. As the war drew to its conclusion, the hard-pressed night fighter pilots realised that they were now making token gestures against an air force that had total air superiority. There was nonetheless honour still at stake, and Schnaufer made it a costly night for the RAF on 7 March. His first sortie brought him two more Lancasters, then, on his second, and in the space of 17 minutes, he accounted for seven more to take his final score to 121, making him the leading night fighter ace of the war.

After the war his Bf 110 was displayed in London and one of its rudders is still on display in the Imperial War Museum in London. Although Heinz Schnaufer survived the war he, like the American ace Dave Schilling, was killed in a motoring accident in France in 1950, at which time he was still only 28 years old.

BIBLIOGRAPHY

*I*t would clearly be impossible to mention every work published that includes some details of aces, the campaigns in which they fought and died, the aircraft they flew and insights into their personal lives. The following are a few that readers will find worthwhile if their appetite has been whetted by this book.

Air Aces, Christopher Shores, Bison Books, London, 1983
Aces High, Alan Clark, Weidenfeld & Nicolson, London, 1973
Battle over Britain, Francis Mason, McWhirter Twins, London, 1969
Aces High, Christopher Shores & Chris Williams, Neville Spearman, London, 1966
The Narrow Margin, Derek Wood & Derek Dempster, Arrow Books, London, 1963
History of the German Air Force, Bryan Philpott, Bison/Hamlyn, London, 1986
Encyclopedia of German Military Aircraft, Bryan Philpott, Arms & Armour Press, London, 1980
The Mighty Eighth, Roger Freeman, Macdonald Janes, London, 1970
Mighty Eighth War Diaries, Roger Freeman, Macdonald Janes, London, 1981
RAF Biggin Hill, Graham Wallace, Tandem Books, London, 1969
Knights of the Iron Cross, Gordon Williamson, Blandford Press, Poole, 1987
Fighter Pilots of the RAF, Chaz Bowyer, Wm Kimber & Co, London, 1984
Fighter Pilots of WW2, Robert Jackson, St Martins Press, New York, 1976
Thunderbolt, Robert Johnson & Martin Caidin, Ballantine Books, New York, 1958
Aircraft versus Aircraft, Norman Franks, Grub Street, London, 1986
Aces & Aircraft of WW 1, Christopher Campbell, Blandford Press, Poole, 1981
They fought for the Sky, Quentin Reynolds, Cassell & Co, London, 1958
Reach for the Sky, Paul Brickhill, Collins, London, 1954
The First & the Last, Adolf Galland, Schneekluth, Darmstadt, Methuen London, 1953
Ginger Lacey – Fighter Pilot, R. T. Bickers, Robert Hale, London, 1966

Ace of Aces, E. C. R. Baker, Wm Kimber & Co, London, 1965

Fighter Exploits, Edward Sims, Corgi Books, London, 1973

Eagle Day, Richard Collier, Hodder & Stoughton, London, 1966

Fighter Pilot, Anon (1941), B. T. Batsford, London, 1941

History of the 9th Air Force, Ken Rust, Aero Publishers Inc, California, 1970

History of the 15th Air Force, Ken Rust, Historical Aviation Album, California, 1975

Marseille – Star of Africa, Heinz Joachim Nowarra, J. W. Caler Corp, California, 1975

Aircam Airwar Series, various authors, Osprey, London, 1977-1980

Luftwaffe Photo-Album Series, Bryan Philpott, Patrick Stephens Limited, Cambridge, 1978-1981

In Enemy Hands, Bryan Philpott, Patrick Stephens Limited, Cambridge, 1981

Duel under the Stars, Wilhem Johnen, Wm Kimber & Co, London, 1969

Fly for your Life, Larry Forrestor, Frederick Muller, London, 1958

Test Pilot, Neville Duke, Allen Wingate, London, 1953

Fighter Command, Chaz Bowyer, J. M. Dent & Sons, London, 1980

The Hardest Day, Dr Alfred Price, Macdonald Janes, London, 1979

History of the RAF, Chaz Bowyer, Hamlyn, London, 1977

INDEX

AIRCRAFT

This section is divided into types by country and name; all variants are included under the indexed name except where identification is by type number only.

UNITS & SQUADRONS

MISCELLANEOUS